THE CHRYSALIS

A Metamorphosis Has Begun!

Robert A. Serocki, Jr.

ONE WORLD PRESS
Chino Valley, Arizona

Copyright © 2014, Robert A. Serocki, Jr.

All rights reserved. No part of this book may be reproduced in any manner without written permission from the publisher, except in the case of quotes used in critical articles and reviews.

ISBN: 978-1-938043-14-7

Book and author information at www.robertserocki.com

Cover Design by Adi Zuccarello, a.zuccarello@gmail.com

Text Design by One World Press, production@oneworldpress.com

This book was published in the USA by:

ONE WORLD PRESS
890 Staley Lane
Chino Valley, AZ 86323
800-250-8171
PrintMyBook@OneWorldPress.com
www.oneworldpress.com

From manuscript to book in 60 days.
www.coachingforpublishers.com

Joshua 1:9 Have I not commanded you? Be strong and courageous. Do not be terrified; do not be discouraged. For the LORD your God will be with you wherever you go.

DEDICATION

This book is dedicated to my father. Thank you for making me strong enough to endure and savvy enough to survive! Love, your son.

"I don't believe I would ever have known how to appreciate the blessing of peace had I not experienced the effects of war!"
Mother Magdalen,
March of 1862,
Loretto Chapel, Santa Fe, New Mexico

"The desire for safety stands against every great and noble enterprise!"
Tacitus

"We have on the contrary, to consider the psychic process as psychic and not as an organic cell process. However indignant people may get about "metaphysical phantoms" when cell-processes are explained vitalistically, they nevertheless continue to regard the physical hypothesis as "scientific," although it is no less fantastic. But it fits in with the materialistic prejudice, and therefore every bit of nonsense, provided that it only turns the psychic into the physical, becomes scientifically sacrosanct. Let us hope that the time is not far off when this antiquated relic of ingrained and thoughtless materialism will be eradicated from the minds of our scientists."
CG Jung from his book, Dreams

ACKNOWLEDGEMENTS

To my good childhood friends Don Vetter and Robert Pierce: Thank you for reviewing my book and/or helping me to spread my message. Most importantly, thank you for always being my true friends. To the gift God has provided me, Bianca Hernandez: Thanks for your support and for taking care of me and for listening to all of my ranting, ravings and pontifications over the years. The 10 years we have known each other is just a drop in the bucket compared to the infinity of life that we will know each other. Love is too simple of a word to describe my feelings.

TABLE OF CONTENTS

Chapter 1 EXORDIUM 1
Chapter 2 PHASE 1 5
Chapter 3 PHASE 2 21
Chapter 4 PHASE 3 27
Chapter 5 PHASE 4 56
Chapter 6 THE BUTTERFLY 78

CHAPTER 1
EXORDIUM

    Thick smoke and the smell of gunpowder filled the late autumn air as our battle lines broke. The smoke was so thick it was hard to see in the woods. We were ordered to retreat and I began running through the woods. Most of the trees were bare as if God had stripped them clean with his hands and dropped the leaves on the ground. They lay there in all of their splendid colors crackling like gunfire under my every footstep.
    My heart is pounding, my breathing heavy and the crisp cold air burns my lungs as I suck it deep into them. My arms are tired and my musket heavy. My heavy woolen coat weighs on me like a boulder on my back. I am sweating profusely and I want to stop running but, I cannot. I am being pursued by three British soldiers. I head for a clearing in the trees where the smoke was not so thick and the air clearer so I could breathe. Once I passed the tree line I looked behind me and everyone was scattered far about accept for the three British soldiers who were pursuing me.
    I kept running as fast as I could, however, being fatigued from the previous battle, I am finding it hard to keep my legs moving. I must stop. The British soldiers are getting closer and I can see

their polished bayonets glistening in the sunlight as if they were salivating just waiting in anticipation for the chance to pierce my gut just like the jowls of a voracious dog waiting to consume a hunk of meat.

I see a small knoll ahead and I decide that this is where I will make my final stand. I lay down behind the knoll and bring my musket to the ready. Just as I aim at one of the British soldiers and prepare to pull the trigger, I hear a crack above my right ear and feel the searing, burning pain of a musket ball enter my chest just below my collar bone. I feel the bone crack and break as I feel the musket ball come out of my back on the right side of my spine, but left of my shoulder blade. The pain was unbearable. I had dropped my musket and was lying in a pool of blood. My breathing got shallow…

◊

The battle lines had been broken. Men were scattering everywhere, running this way and that like ants before a rainstorm. I t was mass confusion. It was hard to tell who was even on whose side with all of the smoke in the air. Bullets were whizzing by every which way. There was nowhere to go to escape. Everywhere I looked Union and Confederate soldiers were fighting and the battle itself was enclosed by sandstone hills and pine trees. I t was complete chaos. Just then, I saw an abandoned wagon on a road nearby. I ran towards it to seek cover from the gunfire.

I peered inside the wagon with my rifle ready; however, no one was inside it. So, I slid open the door to the luggage compartment in the floor of the wagon and I crawled inside and shut the door and decided to wait until the battle was over.

Suddenly, the door slid open and there was a Union soldier standing there with his rifle at the ready and his bayonet inches from my chest. Before I could even take my next breath he rammed his bayonet into my chest and it came out through my back as I heard the crunching of bone and the tearing of my flesh.

I heard and saw the blood gurgle on the blade as he twisted the bayonet and pulled it out...

◊

We had been walking for what seemed like hours since our last firefight. We finally made it out of the jungle into a clearing of tall grass. There were only two of us left, myself and the radio man. I was the platoon sergeant. All of a sudden it began to rain heavily and I looked off into the distance and saw a little house with a thatch roof. I tell my radio man to, "get moving and head for that house so we can get out of the rain for a while." Just then, I hear a crack over my right ear. I feel a bullet strike my back on the right side of my spine between it and my scapula and it came out the middle of my chest. I hit the ground with a thud as blood gurgled in my chest with every listless breath I took as I lie there witnessing my life leaving me...

◊

These three dreams I have just told you repeated themselves to me throughout my childhood and did not stop until I joined the Marines at 18 years of age. I realize this is a rather bold statement of course, but the dreams were telling me that the military and subsequently the war I would end up in, were going to be a big part of my life and become an enemy to me if I did not face it and move beyond it. Hence, running away from my enemy, as I did in my dreams, the war I would become involved in would only kill me by destroying my heart from suffering through life.

Therefore, suggesting I would need to face it in order to survive it and if not it would consume my life. Thereby, suggesting there must be some reason for surviving the war I would undoubtedly face. But, what could that be? Or, is this much too esoteric for our primitive minds, with which we dismiss dreams as nonsensical absurdity. Yet, they comprise half of our life, body, and soul.

It's like CG Jung said in his book, *Dreams*, "Dreams of modern man bring him memories, insights, experiences, awaken dormant qualities in our personality, and reveal the unconscious element in our relationships. So, it seldom happens that anyone who has taken the trouble to work over his dreams with qualified assistance for a longer period of time remains without enrichment and a broadening of his mental horizon." Therefore, I bring you my life.

CHAPTER 2
PHASE 1

As the years of my childhood passed by and I turned into an adult my desire to become a Marine took over my consciousness to the point that I can't stop thinking about it. The day finally came and I was off to boot camp. It was 13 weeks of pure hell. During my tour in the Marine Corps, which lasted four years, I was sent over seas to fight in the first Gulf War. I was there from the beginning until the end. We arrived in Saudi Arabia on August 12, 1990 and we returned home March 30, 1991. I was a combat engineer, which basically means I worked with explosives, booby traps and land mines. The war was pure hell as one could imagine, full of death, blood, suffering, and deceit. It was so bad that I spent the next 20 years of my life in an apathetic, grieving, fearful state. I even wrote a book about those experiences hoping to get some sort of catharsis out of it. I did, however, at that time, I did not realize my work was only beginning. The book is called: ***A line in the Sand: The true experience of a Marine on the front lines of the Gulf War.*** (www.robertserocki.com)

Once I returned from the war, I was picked up at Camp Pendleton by my family and a girl I had been writing to for several months and subsequently fallen in love with her. Her name was April. Of course I had not seen, let alone been with, a woman in a year. We hit it off right away and my parents disliked her immensely. This obviously created a tad bit of turmoil between my parents and me. However, life went on. April and I dated for several months. I would come home to Arizona every weekend I could to see her. We were getting a new Colonel in our battalion in six months, so the Corps gave us a four day pass every weekend. I still; however, had a year left in the Marine Corps.

After several months of dating, I asked April to move out to California with me and she did. We got a one bedroom apartment that was furnished, but so tiny we couldn't pass each other in the hall or the kitchen. It was at this point that we decided to get married. We eloped to Vegas and got married at the "We've only just begun" wedding chapel. That name turned out to be quite ironic.

Once we told my parents, they became quite acrimonious and quit talking to me for about six months. The first few months after we got married seemed to be going along quite fine. We were surviving our small one bedroom apartment and I began talking to my parents again.

However, one day April got mad at me. We were watching America's Most Wanted and I was talking to my step dad on the phone. The TV show started mentioning "bat lady" and how she was wanted for murder and that they called her bat lady because of a ring of bats she had tattooed around her upper arm. Then, they showed her picture. I said, "Holy shit!" It was the girl I had been dating when I first went to Saudi Arabia, who quit writing me in the early days of my deployment and I had never heard from her again.

Of course, April was getting pissed off at me because the woman was rather attractive. She did not know the story. When my step dad hear me say, "Holy shit" he said, "What's the matter?" I said, "I will call you back later I have to go now." I then proceeded to explain the story to my wife at the time and she just got even more pissed because it was a girl I slept with. This I did not understand because I was dating this woman way before I ever met April and it ended before I met April. So, she ended up not talking to me for a week.

Then, one day my First Sergeant calls me in his office and tells me to have a seat. So, I did. He then said, "Serocki, what have you been doing? I know we have only been home several weeks, but what the hell is going on?" I said, "I don't know what you are talking about First Sergeant?" He said, "I just got a phone call from the damn FBI. They want to talk to you. Here's a quarter you go call them and report right back to me immediately." "Aye, aye First Sergeant," I replied.

So, I proceeded to call the FBI. They told me they were looking for a girl named Jackie Caradine, code named the Bat Lady. They told me she was wanted for murder. She pushed a radio into the bathtub of an Army guy while he was taking a bath, which electrocuted and killed him. She also beat an Air force guy over the head with a fire log. I said, "Holy shit: Why the hell are you calling me? I just got home from the war." They explained to me that they found some of my letters in her personal belongings and they thought she might try to get into touch with me. They told me not to speak with her and if I see her, or, if she contacts me I am to call the FBI immediately. I said, "Yes sir!" I then had to return to the First Sergeant's office and explain what had happened. He gave me his home phone number and told me that if I saw her to call him immediately and he would come pick me up, no matter what time of night it was.

Apparently, she was after the $100,000.00 life insurance policy money the spouses receive if their husbands die while on duty in the military. However, each person had to pick a beneficiary who they wanted the money to go to and I had picked my mother because I wasn't married at the time. So, if she would have killed me, she wouldn't have received a damn thing.

Time went on and April and I decided to get a nicer apartment. So, we got a one bedroom apartment for $740.00 a month, which was expensive for 1991. It overlooked the ocean and was next to the freeway. This was convenient because everyone who has ever been to California knows that you can't get anywhere unless you use the freeway.

Once we got into this apartment, things began to get worse and worse between us. I was gone a lot on field missions and had the sneaky suspicion she was cheating on me. I also found out that this young lady had quite the temper. Every time she would get mad at me she would hit me in the mouth. So, I would flip her on the ground and hold her there until she calmed down. Until one time she said she was calm and I let her up off of the floor and she went into the kitchen and got a butcher knife and came after me. I quickly reacted, due to my Marine combat training. I knocked the knife out of her hand and punched her in the chest. She fell to the floor gasping for air. Almost a year later, I decided to divorce her. I only had a couple of months left in the Marines and I had planned to move back to Michigan, which is where my father was living.

Upon arriving in Michigan on August 1st of 1992, my father told me I had a phone call from April. Our divorce wasn't set to go through until November of that year, so I was wondering what in the hell she was calling me for. So, I called her and she proceeded to tell me she was pregnant and that the baby was mine. I told her she was full of it and it had to be one of her boyfriend's and I hung up on her.

Well, time went by and December rolled around. It was Christmas season, which is the season of love, joy and peace for all! So, I started feeling guilty about the baby situation with April and I called her to see how she was doing. She, of course, told me she was still pregnant and the baby was definitely mine and that she would send me pictures of herself. So, she did and she was definitely pregnant. I decided to fly out to Arizona where she was living. My mother and step dad also lived there. I stayed with them while I was visiting. I figured that she couldn't lie to me to my face. I had to confront her.

So, I took a weeks' vacation from my job working at a robotics factory in Detroit, Michigan. I was doing pretty well there. I got paid every week and I was living at my dad's house in the basement, so I was saving money like crazy. I flew out to Arizona to check on the situation.

When I finally saw April she was definitely pregnant. She still was saying to my face that the baby was mine. I could not help having feelings for her and the child. I knew that I had to quit my job in Detroit and move back to Arizona in order to take care of my responsibilities.

I went back to Detroit and told my dad I was moving back to Arizona and why. He got pissed and told me I was being stupid and the baby wasn't mine. However, I had to do what I had to do and he could not understand that at the time. I packed my stuff and left. I drove back to Arizona.

I was living with my mother and step dad. Several weeks went by and it was time for the baby to be delivered. I went to the hospital and when it was time to actually give birth I was there with April holding her hand.

I watched as the doctor botched the episiotomy. They had to cut April four different ways to get the baby's head out. I stood there and watched blood squirt out half way across the room because the doctor cut one of her arteries.

Finally, the baby was delivered. I cut the umbilical cord and saw the placenta as the doctor set it in the stainless steel pan next to me. I then held the baby and cried at what an amazing thing I had just witnessed. I gave April a kiss and told her she did a good job even though she yelled and screamed at me the whole time she was giving birth.

We were finally able to take the baby home. I spent every day of that next week with April helping with the baby. April had developed a high fever and I had to take her back to the hospital to get a blood transfusion because she lost so much blood during child birth.

After she got well she stated acting funny. She did not want to see me as much or let me hold the baby. One time, while I was there she got mad and punched me in the mouth like she used to do when we were married.

One Friday night my mother and step dad wanted to go out to the bar and asked me to watch my nine year old half-sister. I was 22 at the time. I said I would do that. While I was babysitting her April had called me on the phone and we got into an argument. I had raised my voice during our conversation. So, when my step dad came home, without my mother because she wanted to stay at the bar and get drunk of course, my sister proceeded to tell my step dad that I was screaming and yelling and slammed the phone down and that she got scared and had to hide in her room. Which was quite and embellished story and typical of a spoiled rotten nine year old.

So, I was sitting on one couch, my step dad on the other. He started yelling at me and I told him that I did get into an argument with April, but it was not like Carlie had said. He did not believe me. I said, "You are actually going to believe a nine year old kid over a 22 year old adult?" He said, "Yes." Of course, he had been drinking at the bar along with my mother so his thought process and logic were most likely quite convoluted.

He then jumped up off the couch and came after me. In a split second, the time that he and my mother beat me with a PVC pipe, broke my finger, and beat me with other various cooking implements in high school, ran through my mind. Then, all of a sudden, once again, my training as a Marine suddenly kicked in. My step dad pushed me and as he did I grabbed his arms and flipped him over the couch and grabbed him by the throat and with my right arm cocked and ready to punch him in the throat. I then told him, "I am not a little boy anymore and if you ever touch me like that again I will kill you!"

I got up and went to bed leaving him lye on the floor and think about what he had just done. I had to get up at 5am to go to work. I had acquired a job waiting tables at a local restaurant and I had to work the breakfast shift the next morning.

I went to work and came home around 1pm to find all of my stuff packed and on the porch. My step dad opened the front door and said, "Your mother wants you out of this house!" He then closed and locked the door. My mother didn't show her face of course. She most likely was hung over again. I grabbed all of my stuff and loaded it into my truck. I did not have anywhere to go, so I was not sure what to do.

My youngest uncle rented a room in a house with some other people. So, I went to his house and told him what was going on. I called his older brother, who was a role model to me, but he blamed everything on me. I asked my youngest uncle if I could take showers at his house so I don't have to go to work dirty. He said that I could. I was living out of my truck so he also let me sleep on his couch for the time being.

Tips weren't very good where I was working, but it was a job. It took me about a month to save up enough money to rent a room in a house, which turned out to be a meth house. I did not figure that out until I moved in. I worked almost every day of the week and did a lot of double shifts so I did not have to spend much time in the house I was living in.

After about a month of this, April called me and told me that the baby wasn't mine and that she did it all just to piss me off! After that, I never heard from her again. I was completely devastated that a human being could do such a thing. I wanted to go kick her ass, but my roommate at the time had stopped me from leaving the house. I did not know what else to do so I got drunk.

Some time had passed and while I was still living in the meth house, we got a new roommate named Elana. She and I hit it off and we started dating. She had a pierced tongue, belly button ring, and numerous tattoos. She wasn't really my type, but at this point in my life I didn't really care. She liked me when no one else did.

The meth house really began to get on my nerves. One day I came home from work and found my roommate doing a drug deal in her room. She had a one year old son whom she had out in the back yard by himself while she was, shall we say, conducting her business in her bedroom. I yelled d down the hall to inquire about just who was watching the baby. She said that she was through the window. I then asked her, "What are you going to do if he falls down and busts his head open, jump through the window?" She then came storming down the hallway and went out into the back yard and picked up the baby and brought him in the house and dropped him into my lap and said, "Here, if your so concerned you watch him!"

She became pissed off about that and the next day, when she was high of course, she was passing me in the hallway and she shoved me and started yelling at me. I grabbed her by her shirt and slammed her into the wall knocking the wind out of her and I told her not to touch me again or she would surely get an ass whooping like she's never had before, but definitely needed, and I walked away.

On top of these incidents I watched her neglect her child while she would get high and stay up for three days and then sleep for three days. I watched her finally eat something only to go throw it up seconds later because her boyfriend liked her skinny, seeing her with soars all over her face and her teeth falling out in pieces, smelling the meth as it oozed from her pores, and having thugs and criminals with guns constantly coming in and out of the house, I decided I had to move.

By this time, I was talking to my family again, only because I apologized for what happened even though I was defending myself. I started a landscaping business with Elana's mother and got a job at a local bank as a bill collector. With all three jobs, landscaping, the restaurant, and the bank, I was working 96 hours a week without ever having a day off for an entire year. I had to get the hell out of that house!

I finally saved enough money to rent out a house. So I rented a house and then rented out all of the rooms so I would be living there for free. It was a decent four bedroom house. Elana came with me and so did one of my friends.

It was at this point that my relationship with Elana started to deteriorate. We started arguing a lot. One time a roommate moved out and we were about to get a new one and one of Elana's cats had pissed all over the couch in the family room and it stunk like hell. So, we got into an argument about who was going to clean it up before the new roommate moved in. I certainly wasn't going to do it. It wasn't my cat!

She subsequently stormed down the hallway and went into our bedroom and slammed the door so hard it broke the door jamb so it was stuck shut. I could hear her in the room beating on the door. So, I went down the hall and told her to knock it off because I would have to pay for the damage. I tried to go into the room, but the door wouldn't open. I finally forced it open and she was standing right there ready to kick me in the groin. I pushed her back and told her to calm the hell down.

I went back out into the family room and I heard her on the phone telling someone I had her pinned down to the bed and that I was beating her, which obviously was not true. I thought she was talking to her dad who also used to be a Marine and I thought for sure he was coming over and I would have to kick his ass.

As soon as she got off of the phone she left the house and left the front door wide open. I called my step dad and told him that we got into an argument and I asked if I could come to his house and stay there for the night until Elana calmed down. He said that I could. I sat down to finish watching Star Trek and then I was going to leave when all of a sudden, five cops came running into the house with their guns drawn.

I jumped up off of my chair and said, "What the hell:" One of the cops said, "Calm down son, calm down." I said, "When five cope come running into my house with their guns drawn, I am going to get a little excited!" One of the cops talked to me about what happened and one of them went to check the bedroom and he saw the door jamb broken from when she slammed the door and a hole in the door that had been there from the previous owners.

The cop then said, "How'd this hole get here?" I explained to him that it had been there since we moved in and he said, "It looks to me like you kicked it in." I replied, "Well, I didn't. If you're so smart, you should have been an engineer instead of a cop!" It was at that point that the police went outside to talk to Elana. They talked to her for five minutes and came back in the house and arrested me.

As we were walking down the driveway the cop stopped me and asked me if I had anything to say to Elana. I said, "You guys better make sure her and all of her stuff is out of here by the time I get out of jail in the morning or you will have a reason to come back!"

The cop put me in the car and explained to me that he knew I didn't hurt her, but because of my military record in the Marines, of which he had rattled off all of my medals, the sniper training I had received, and the war I was in, he said, "He had to take me to jail because I was a bigger threat." I asked the cop what I should do and he said, "Plead not guilty and they will let you out in the morning and you will have to go to an anger management course. You already did the right thing by getting rid of your girlfriend before we took you to jail. So, everything will work out." I said, "Ok" and spent a lovely night in jail with the local drunks, meth addicts, and the indigent people who inhabited our city. Once I got out of jail, I went to the Vet Center and talked to a counselor. The counselor called the County Attorney and the charges were eventually dropped and I had a clean slate.

After that incident, life moved on for me. I ended up moving into a duplex that friends of my parents owned with another roommate. I did not have any money so they charged me cheap rent as long as I took care of any maintenance issues for the duplex.

It was at this point that my Post Traumatic Stress Disorder (PTSD) really started bothering me. However, I did not know what was wrong. I drank a lot to numb myself from the god awful memories I \had from the war, from killing a man and seeing numerous bodies and body parts blown all over the desert, and from my abusive and violent childhood. I felt like I was mad all of the time, but I didn't know why. I would go out to bars and get drunk and start my own war to work out my frustrations not knowing what I was really doing. I slept with my bed against the wall, I was scared of the dark, I sat in corners with my back to the wall, and I jumped and shook from loud noises, all at the age of 26.

It was at this point, that I got into bull riding. Probably the most dangerous thing I could have ever done except go to war. But, I was doing it because of just that. It was dangerous. I could get injured or even die going to work. I saw blood and broken bones. These things were all things that I was familiar with. This was an environment I was able to function in. It was like being at war and that was the only way I knew how to live.

Once I decided to get out of the Marines, they just let me go. No one taught me how to be human again. No one taught me how to be a productive part of society. No one taught me that I can't start a war every time I got drunk. I was left to fend for myself like an animal. I felt like someone had thrown me, all covered in blood, into an ocean full of man eating sharks and it was a gamble to stay alive. All I knew was war. All I had were its memories, which caused me to drink myself into oblivion to numb the emotional effects of what I saw and did. All of the blood, death and killing. The emotional baggage that these events brought with them haunted me every day and they continued to get worse.

One of the rodeos I went to was in Durango, Mexico. It was the USA against Mexico. It was a lot of fun. The people there were very generous and kind. I got invited to go because I was at a bar one night that had bull riding. I was there with some of my riding buddies, which included Elana, who was now my ex-girlfriend. We were riding bulls at the bar there that night.

It was my turn to ride and I had my partner pull my rope tight and I tied my hand into the suitcase handle of the rope. Elana told me good luck and I scooted up on the rope, shook my head and said, "Ok boys, let's go!" The shoot gate opened up and the bull blew straight up in the air and he jumped a couple of times and ran straight for the corner of the arena, which is where he bucked me off and subsequently stepped on my calf. That was the second time that happened to me that week. I couldn't get up at first. But, I finally was able to hobble out of the arena.

When I got back behind the chutes I laid down on the ground and started cussing like crazy because of the pain. I asked my rodeo partner to lift up my pant leg and make sure I was not bleeding. I wasn't, but it hurt like hell. After the rodeo, which is a common practice, we went into the bar. It was here that we were approached by a Mexican cowboy to come ride in a rodeo down in Durango, Mexico. He told us they would take care of everything except for our entry fees. There were five of us. We said ok. I was still in pain with my leg, but the beer was slowly helping with that. My leg was black and blue from my knee to my toes. It was so swollen that it looked like I had no ankle and no toes!

By the time we got to Mexico my leg was killing me. But, I had to ride. I could not show the others I was in pain. After all, I was a rookie and had to prove myself.

I had some fun down there in good 'ol Mexico. They closed off the main street in town and the locals made us stop at every restaurant for food and beer, which they gave us all for free, and we rode a mechanical bull in the street. It was a giant party. I got bucked off both Friday and Saturday nights and got to see Elana sleep with one of the other cowboys. I just drank and tried to pretend that nothing bothered me.

I rode bulls in the rodeo for three years until one day I really got hurt. It's not if you get hurt bull riding, it's when. Then, one day, I drew a small bull. If there is such a thing. I am tall for a bull rider, about six feet. My feet could just about touch each other underneath its belly. The bull came out and spun to the right one time. It pulled the upper half of my body down towards its head and spun around again. Only this time, when it pulled me down, his head was waiting for me! He turned his head and horned me in the chin. The impact knocked me out cold. I bounced off of the bull's head five or six times while he kept spinning. I then fell to the ground and the bull proceeded to step all over my body because my hand was hung up in the rope and I was still unconscious.

The rodeo clown got my hand out of the rope and they got the bull away from me and stopped the rodeo. Those guys are the real athletes! They saved my life. I was still unconscious and choking on my tongue. The rodeo clown put his finger in my mouth to get my tongue out and I finally came to and awoke. The first thing I did was say, "Get your freaking hands off of me!" I had amnesia for about 20 minutes or so, my chin was split wide open, my wrist was broken and my ribs were cracked. Needless to say, that ended my career as a bull rider.

I went back to landscaping but, I was bored with mowing grass and trimming trees and I wanted more out of life. I decided to go to college. I went to college because I was going to expand my landscaping business. So, I registered to get a degree in landscaping architecture. In the beginning, I was just taking some of the required math, English, and science classes. One of the classes I had was an art history class. Right off of the bat we started learning about Egypt and its rich cultural history. It was right then and there that I decided I was going to be an archaeologist.

I proceeded to go back down to the advisor's office that day and completely rearranged my schedule so that I could get a degree in anthropology. In the meantime, my mother had called me and told me about this museum my sister had gone to and she gave me their phone number and told me to call them for a job. I held onto the number for two weeks because I didn't know anything about archaeology yet and did not think I could get a job.

However, because it was eating away at me, I decided to call the museum to find out how I could break into the business of archaeology. They told me that they actually had a position open and it wasn't archaeology per say, but it would get my feet wet. So, I rushed down there and filled out the application and eventually got a job working at the front desk greeting museum patrons and cleaning toilets.

Things were exciting. I was learning about archaeology and doing a little bit of it too. But, my PTSD became worse. It took every ounce of energy I had to go to school and to work. I would come home and have to drink just to calm down and feel numb. I would spend the entire time in class sitting in the corner by the door planning how I was going to get out of there if anything happened. I wasn't able to concentrate on what my professors were saying. I had to bring a tape recorder with me to record the lectures so I could review them at home and study.

While I was in college I worked two jobs and went to school full time. I was working so hard that I finally became dehydrated to the point my electrolytes were so screwed up that I passed out in a restaurant and my heart had stopped beating for an entire minute. When I awoke on the floor of the hospital, the paramedic was standing over me getting ready to jam an adrenaline needle right through the center of my chest into my heart. I also had a seizure. That made me quit drinking alcohol and caffeine for an entire year. However, the panic attacks were relentless and I absolutely couldn't take it anymore and I started drinking again just so I could have a brief moment of peace at the end of my day.

Time went by and I started dating a girl I met in school in one of my anthropology classes. While I was dating her, I developed more severe panic attacks and I was even afraid to leave my house! I had her go to the grocery store for me to buy food because I physically couldn't do it and I was deathly afraid to get stuck in a long line and be trapped. I was scared to death to go to work and school. However, I knew I had to do those things if my life was going to get any better. Besides, when I got home I could just drink my problems away.

As time went on, I was still dating the girl I met in college and I finally graduated and got a full time job with the museum that I had been working for, which was operated by the local public municipality. My girlfriend was putting up with my panic attacks, drinking, and my PTSD. We decided to get engaged to get married and I went and bought a house nestled in the desert foothills at the base of a mountain. It was a little 1140 square foot condo for us when we finally got married.

One night, her and I were at the local bar that I used to walk to from the condo and I got so drunk that when it was time to go I fell down the stairs at the bar entrance. We continued walking home down this unlit road through the desert down a hill. The road made a right turn and I fell and rolled all the way down the hill until I was stopped by a Jumping Cholla cactus! Needless to say, my fiancé was absolutely furious with me.

We never did actually get married because of my panic attacks. I didn't know what was wrong and I thought I was going crazy. Drinking was the only thing that kept me sane, until the next morning when it would bring my panic attacks back with a vengeance. It was a vicious cycle. My fiancé and I finally broke up after five years of dating and I was now alone in this house trying to find a way to afford it on my meager salary. There were days when I couldn't afford to turn on the heat so I sat in front of the oven with blankets on. There were also days in the summer when I couldn't turn the air conditioning on when it was 115 degrees outside. I would just sit as long as I could in the community pool.

While I was still living in this house, I met another girl, Francine, through work. She worked for one of the environmental firms in town. We fell in love, or so I thought, and became engaged three months later. Several months after that we found out she was pregnant. It was fine with me. We both had decent jobs and medical insurance and we were engaged to be married.

One night we were sitting on our porch and out of the blue she told me I was crazy from the war. I said, "I don't know what you are talking about. What do you want me to do?" She then said she knew I was crazy because she talked to her cousin who was in Viet Nam and he is crazy now. I said, "I am not your cousin!"

She finally told me that she wanted me to see a therapist. So, I agreed since I could see one through my benefits package at work for free. I asked her to come with me so she could explain to the therapist what my problems were because I had no idea what she was talking about. She said she would, but she never did. I still went to the first appointment and the therapist talked to me for quite a while and I scheduled a second appointment. This time, I asked Francine to make me a list of my problems so I could show them to the therapist so we would have something to discuss. She said she would, but again, she did not.

So, I went to my second appointment and the first words out of the therapists' mouth were, "Where is your fiancé? Why didn't she come with you? Did she make you a list of the issues for you?" I answered "no" to all of her questions. She then asked me about the last 10 years of my life and so I told her. The therapist told me that I was not crazy and it was my fiancé and her mother that needed the services of a good therapist, not me. When I got home that evening my fiancé asked about the therapist appointment and

I told her it went fine. I did not want to tell her what she really said because I knew that would launch her into a vigorous rage.

A few weeks later we were sitting on the couch and all of a sudden she started crying and said, "Tell me everything is going to be better." I had no idea what was wrong with her so I called my mom and she said, "It's just her hormones from being pregnant."

One night, on my way home from work I decided I was going to cook a dinner high in folic acid, because I knew it was good for the baby. I called Francine from the grocery store and told her what I was going to do. She said she was at her mom's, but I could still make it for the next day. So, I decided to get the stuff and make my homemade spaghetti for her.

I went home and sat there and waited for her to come home for three hours. It was now nine at night and I was starving and I had not heard from her. I went to the local tavern by the condo and had dinner. When I got home two hours later, some of her things were missing, like toiletries, etc. There was no note, no nothing to let me know what was going on and where she was. I tried calling her but got no answer. Francine was now gone pregnant with my son and I didn't know what the hell was going on. I was furious. I finally went to bed and tried to sleep, but I couldn't.

The next morning she called me and said she had to leave because I was crazy, but it was not her intention to end the relationship. I said, "Well, you just took off with our baby and abandoned me without trying to work anything out. It's over. Come and get your stuff out of my house!" She said, "I tried talking with you, but it didn't work." I replied, "Telling me twice that I am crazy and not even going to the therapist with me is not trying to work things out. We are done. Come and get your stuff or I will throw it all out in the street!"

She finally came and got her stuff and I did not hear from her for nine months. I knew that I would hear from her then because she would want money! And that is exactly what happened.

CHAPTER 3
PHASE 2

It was Christmas time and the time of year when my uncles and I would make our yearly journey up to some cabins in the forest the day after Christmas. We would go up North and explore the outdoors, fish and at night we would drink and talk shit in the local tavern like guys do. I would talk about my life, plans I had, and dreams I wished I could fulfill. We would tell old family stories and stories from each of our childhoods. It was a great time. It was my favorite time of the year.

We would leave the day after Christmas and stay for the next two nights doing our thing and bonding. After, we would come back from the restaurant/bar, my oldest uncle would go to bed and the other one and I would stay up and watch TV for a while until we fell asleep. It was at this time that I developed very vivid symbolic dreams, which I was tormenting myself over, trying to interpret them. I wrote every single one of them down in a journal as soon as I woke up thinking someday I would use them for something.

Dream: 12/28/03 I was walking through a busy downtown area with someone I knew. It was a woman.

I got captured by these priests whose eyes glowed. They wore big silver crosses around their necks. They captured me and whomever I was with and put us on top of a four story building, which was in front of a church. I could see through the walls of the church. It also had for floors. There were people sitting cross legged, hands clasped together, bibles on the floor in front of them and they were praying. They all looked just like the priests, except the ones on the top floor, they looked like normal people. Then the floors would drop down one floor and the floor on the bottom went underground. The normal people on the top floor turned into the priests once their floor dropped to the next lower floor. As this occurred a new floor appeared on top and the priests would put the people they captured on this floor. I then knew this same thing was going to happen to me. I wanted to jump but I couldn't move and I knew I would not survive the fall. It was like a very powerful force held me there. I tried desperately to brake free. Finally, someone I knew came along on the street up to the building I was on top of. The person helped me down and we took off running. The priests with the glowing eyes followed.

I then woke up in the morning and my uncle who was sleeping on the cabin floor across from me told me that while I was sleeping I had my arms crossed on my chest and my hands by my neck. He said my arms were white and my face was red. He then asked me if I had a dream that I was choking. I said no and told him about my dream.

There are many references in this dream to spirituality, the quaternary, my sensitive side, and my soul, such as the woman I was walking with, the four floors, priests with glowing eyes, the church and the cross. This dream was telling me that I was separated from my sensitive side, thus my soul and spirit, and that I was trying to stay separated from it; however, the natural cycle of things is such that as things get worse, or as things happen to us, we find enlightenment through suffering. No matter how much I resist or where I go, spirit will be with me as it is part of me and it goes wherever I go and I am never really completely separated from it.

A few days had passed by and I was back at my condo I owned in the desert. It was now New Year's Eve and I spent the evening getting drunk at the local pub that I could walk to from my house. I spent most weekends there. I knew the staff and all the regulars, which I was now one of. They were my family. They accepted me just the way I was, Marine and all. That night, when I went to sleep, I said my prayers and asked for knowledge and help interpreting my dreams.

> Dream: 12/31/03 A friend had become ill and I had to take him to the hospital, but he wouldn't cooperate. I was carrying him out to a helicopter but the helicopter took off and left us there. Then we checked my friend into the hospital. Then, I became sick and had to go into the hospital for tests for two weeks. I was waiting for a nurse. My family was there. I opened up the toilet and inside was orange mush and I quickly closed the lid. This big fat nurse came and checked me into a room that had four people in it. She said she couldn't give me my own room because she did not know me that well let and she sat on the bed and leaned against me smothering me. There was also a machine they needed for me, but it broke. Then, someone came to fix it and then someone was taking me through doors and showing me things.

Again, my dreams were telling me that something was wrong with me. That there were things in my past I had to deal with. This dream in particular, is telling me that subconsciously I wanted help; however, I was repressing it. It also foretells me finally breaking down and getting sick and ending up in a hospital for two weeks, which I did nearly six years later! After breaking down and a suicidal ideation I checked into a hospital on 4/23/09 and remained there for two weeks. The dream also told me that I had repressed the fact that I wanted my parents there, but since we had not been on speaking terms for nearly three years they were not. The dream goes on to tell me that I was scared of what I had buried inside me and I did not want to face it (the orange stuff in the toilet and then closing the lid).

In the hospital, I eventually ended up in a few years later, I was in a room with another person and the building was set up like a dorm. It housed many patients in that particular area. It made me feel suffocated because no one could get out. It was sort of like being in jail. The dream told me that eventually, I would break down there and that the staff would begin to h help me step by step and piece by piece, a and they would show me the path to recovery.

My own personal illness was edified in this dream. My illness was the illness of a friend in the dream. I was trying to help my friend. Thus, the dream was telling me that I needed to help myself. No one could do it for me. If they did, I would only reject it and accomplish nothing. Like I said, the dream did predict that I would end up in a hospital. It also said that there is, let's say, a poison inside me (the orange mush in the toilet) that needs to be dealt with, or, removed. It also foretells me going through many more trials and tribulations (the end of the dream with the nurse, the room, her smothering me, and the broken machine). It also predicted that I would find my way and move forward, that life would "open" up to me (the staff taking me through doors and showing me things).

However, I would not realize this until years later. Therefore, things, at that particular time, seemed pretty bleak for me. One night, a few days later, when I went to bed, I was saying my prayers and I asked God to help me interpret my dreams. Especially, the dreams I was having about my last two girlfriends. I knew that they had to have some sort of significance, but I could not figure out just what that was.

Dream: 1/05/03 I was on a bus fleeing from some place that was under attack. The driver drove us somewhere down by the water on a pier where people were parachuting and he shot them out of the sky. Then someone shot him and the bus drove off of the end of the pier and crashed into the water. Before we got on the bus people took things they wanted, but the person in charge said no alcohol, which I did not take. Then we realized we were all going to die on the bus. We would run out of air. I knew one woman on the bus. We said our good byes and that we love each other and we then ran out of air and died. Everything went black.

Then, all of a sudden, I felt like I was slammed back into my body. I awoke and some man was sitting on my night stand next to me. I was startled and swung my hand at him and he disappeared. I was now fully awake with my heart pounding. I then looked on my night stand and I had left a picture there of one of my ex-girlfriends (Mary, whom I was engaged to when I bought the condo in the desert foothills) sitting on the end of the pier in San Clemente, California earlier that day.

My unconscious, my soul, the anima as Jung called it, was telling me time was running out. That I would not have forever to face the problems I had, which I was covering up with drinking. The girl, again according to Jung, reflected my soul, the other half of my whole person. She was representing the fact that if I did not make peace with what was bothering me, that my conscious half of me would end up saying good bye to my soul, my spiritual –part of myself and I would become spiritually dead. In essence, I would become half of a man. A little more simplistically speaking, the dream was telling me that the old girlfriends and alcohol was the end of an "era", so to speak, and that I needed to leave those things in the past and "move forward."

So, interestingly enough, the request I placed before God, when I went to bed that night, was answered! I soon fell back asleep and I had yet another dream.

I dreamt that I was walking around a shopping mall with friends and we each had an alcoholic drink in hand. We were all drunk. I would pass my uncle in the mall a lot. Each time I passed him had a glass of wine in his hand and he was drunk. We then passed some people who made fun of my Grandma. My uncle asked me and my real dad to stop them. They were Indians. We went to fight them and a crowd gathered. A TV fell off of a wall and almost hit this cop in the head. Then the whole thing broke up and I woke up.

This dream obviously was bringing my biggest problem to my attention yet again. It was telling me that I needed to stop self-medicating with the alcohol. The reason my uncle was in the dream is rather poignant. He himself, was an alcoholic. It destroyed his life and his athletic career during the time he drank. In other words, if I did not straighten myself out, I would surely suffer the same fate.

CHAPTER 4
PHASE 3

    A month had passed by and I was sitting in my chair by my dining room window and I had just got off of the phone with my ex fiancé, Francine, who told me she was going to have our baby boy in three days. They were going to perform a "C" section on her. I had not heard from her in nine months, which, as I mentioned before, was what I had expected to happen. I was sitting there contemplating what my life was going to be like now. I was sure she would take me to court and try to take me for everything I had. I also had to make sure that I was a part of my son's life. I wondered about everything. I was scared. I had no idea what the future held for me, on top of the problems I already had.

    Just then, as I was sitting in my chair, that inner voice in my head spoke to me. It said that it was God and that this was the beginning. I would lose everything. My family, my friends, my house, everything; however, it would be ok. It was necessary. It was the path I needed to take. In other words, there would be a death and rebirth of the whole me. Jung galled this the "individuation," or the "complete actualization of the whole human being." I just needed to trust that this was true and follow the path set before me knowing that these things would occur!

The feeling that overcame me was so intense that I started to cry uncontrollably. The presence I felt was very powerful and I was awestruck by it. In fact, I was so moved by the whole experience that I called my mother and told her what had just happened and I had a hard time telling her because I couldn't stop crying.

I hung up the phone and sat there wondering, was this really what was going to happen to me? Would I really lose everything? How would that be ok? Did God really just speak to me? Maybe, I didn't know.

Just then, I was reminded that a few months back, in desperation, I prayed to God and told him I was ready to do his work. I would do whatever he needed me to do. I would serve whatever purpose he needed me to serve. I was tired of being miserable. I wanted to be with him, to walk with him, to be one with him. At that precise moment a chill had just run down my spine. Was it really happening? Now way... couldn't be.

> Dream: 1/06/04 When I went to bed and said my prayers last night, I asked for guidance on what to do about Francine. I dreamt I was at a hotel for a friend's wedding and we were trying to pick out what I should wear. I picked a nice pressed white shirt. My friend said it was too plain. I showed him a bright orange shirt, which he said was to bright. Nothing was good enough so I just stood there and didn't say a word. Then, we were playing baseball and my friend bragged about hitting a home run and on the next at bat he wanted to hit a double and then popped out. I then had to pitch to this girl. She was rather obnoxious. I grabbed the ball with the proper grip, got ready to pitch and she would lose her patience and get upset and walk out of the batter's box. After doing that a few times the umpire threw her out of the game. I ran into her later and smiled and she was upset because I had

beaten her so easily without doing a thing. She did all the work herself.

This dream was telling me that I needed balance in my life (the plain white shirt and the bright orange shirt). I also was being told that nothing I could ever do would be good enough for Francine. It was also telling me that in any interactions I would have with her I would need to keep my mouth shut, in other words, not throw the pitch like in my dream and that she would do all the work herself and things would eventually work out for me. In other words, I was actually in control. It was up to me on how to handle it.

> 1/07/04 I asked God who my next girlfriend would be and when I would meet her, but I wanted it to be the one I am supposed to be with the rest of my life. I dreamt I went to a convenience store to get food for my flight. I bought a lot of chocolate, a chocolate bar and a hot dog. I got to the airport and I was walking with a woman. Someone came up to us and asked if we were from the museo (Spanish for museum) she said yes. The woman with me was working on her degree in college, smaller than me, with dark hair that was pulled back. We then went to check in and I had my acoustic guitar. We had trouble checking it in. I forgot it at the counter and they didn't believe it was mine. The woman I was with said it was mine and that I used to be a colonel in the military and they gave me my guitar and we went to another counter to check in and I woke up.

It was about six months later that I met this Hispanic woman, named Frida at the museum where I worked. She was dark skinned, always had her hair pulled back and to this day, is still working on her college degree. The dream also tells me that she would respect my military service, what I did serving my country and that she had a "high" respect for that (the fact that she said I was a Colonel in the military, which is a very high rank). It also tells me that we would have some difficulties and we would have to "change direction" so to speak, but things would work out (the guitar and having to go to another counter to check in). We have been together nine and a half years now and she has been through everything with me, every step of the way. God could not have made a kinder person.

> 1/08/04 I asked God if I should ask this girl out. I was in a costume pulling a wagon down the canal and my coat opened and a bunch of booze bottles fell out. Then I ran into a girl from work. I was taking a bunch of stuff somewhere. She was going to help me. The people that dressed me up did not come. Then I wanted to ask her out but, a bunch of people and the mayor showed up. He made us all get in a circle and do pushups and hold in place for a camera. I was tired but there was an old man there that was doing it and if he could do it, I could do it. The veins in the old man's biceps were bulging out.

The dream was telling me that I was keeping my issues hidden from this girl, but it would eventually come out (the booze bottles and coat) and thus, not work out for her and I. Moreover, the important thing here, is that the dream was calling my attention to a much bigger issue. The fact that I needed to quit covering up my problems. I needed to face them, deal with them, and get healthy again (getting in a circle and doing pushups). People before me had been through these things and healed from their experiences, moved on and became well. If they could do it, I most certainly could (the old man there doing it and his veins bulging out).

> 1/12/04 I was outside by a busy street playing baseball, while working. There were kids there. I would make sure they all got across the street safely. There was a white car that would come around the

corner very fast and almost hits the kids. It had four people in it, kids who were punks. I was batting and I hit a foul tip and the ball hit me in the gut. It hurt and the ball was going very fast. The ball was pink and distorted. I walked the ball back to the pitcher. He thought I was going to hit him. I just handed him the ball and walked back to the plate. I said, "That's how you take a freaking pitch!" Everyone was in amazement that I took that pitch and did not even flinch. My grandma was sitting by a car. She was laughing and happy. I woke up.

This dream is foretelling that I would eventually be in a place where I was helping people. However, there would also be people there who were trying to hurt everyone else. I also would be suffering from my own issues and that the only way I could help these people is by leading by example and teaching them. It also told me that at that point my family would be happy for me.

1/21/04 I was at a lake fishing. The water was somewhat clear. I could see the fish. Two fat black men were swimming where I was fishing. One jumped on a raft and I said, "Wow, look at him go." I jumped in the water and swam. I got tangled in the fishing line but got out. I caught some fish. I was cleaning them. The insides were dirty. There were big fish floating. They were dead and half cleaned. I said, "What a waste, someone did not use all of the meat." Then I ran into these old people on a boat. I went with them. They asked me to look at their pool skimmer. It was bent when I extended it. Then, I was under a dock cleaning a big fish. An old man gave me another knife. The fish was full of sea weed. The old man then showed me how to fish in the dark brown water that was full of very tall seaweed. We swam in it. These guys in boats and grey storm trooper suits were coming after me. I swam under water through the seaweed to get away. The next thing I know, I am in my dad's bathroom finger banging this really hot blonde and trying to talk her into having sex with me. She is going for it. Then, another woman walks in and says she needs to go to the bathroom, but she did not notice what we were doing. I woke up and then fell back asleep. I then had another dream.

    I dreamt I was with my ex-wife April in a new apartment and we were trying to work things out. We would have sex but only to the point that she would have an orgasm and be satisfied and then get up out of the bed. She would never show she really cared for me. So I tried to have sex with her one more time before work and she quit before I had an orgasm, but she had one. I was late for work. I was trying to finish by jacking off in front of the fire place and two girls walked in, but they did not see me. One of them said, "That's the wood rack we got her for Christmas." I said, "Oh yeah." And they teased me about forgetting already. Then one of the girls and I happened to both live in the same apartment complex and we realized we were late for work. We both decided we would say there was an accident in front of our complex. I was running for my car and my phone rang. It was my dad who was my boss and he thought I wasn't coming to work. I told him I was stuck in accident traffic like the other girl and we would eventually be in. He did not know we both lived in the same complex. He then said, "When I am rich my driver can drive us both around." I said, "Yeah, I would be in in 10 minutes, as soon as I could find my car. But I could not find it and I woke up.

    1/26/04 I was back in the revolutionary war. I was in charge. I was giving orders to new recruits whom were all very young. I was talking to them about either being a walking soldier or in the artillery. One kid passed out. I then focused in on a woman who was in the artillery. She had a wound over her right eye and forehead from an artillery explosion. I was instructing the American troops, but this British officer kept coming up to me on his horse and telling me how to properly make my tea.

The interesting thing about this dream was that it references the revolutionary war. I discussed this earlier in the book when I talked about three re-occurring war dreams I had throughout my childhood, until I actually went into the Marines, went to war and survived. I cannot help but again contemplate the fact that there is a bit of truth to this dream, like the others, and that it is also part of a repertoire of memories I still retain from past lives.

Moreover, I conducted some research and found out that during the revolutionary war, women were often used in artillery units because the men were sent to fight. I also discovered that a common injury for the artillery personnel was facial wounds because the canons did explode from time to time when the fuse was lit! These were things I never knew until I completed my research. In other words, I had information given to me in my dreams that I never knew were actual facts until it was confirmed through the aforementioned research!

2/28/04 I was in the hospital with a bum leg. My whole family was there. They took me up to my room. It was very nice. It had a TV and two queen size beds. I looked out the window and saw a family with kids. It was my ex-wife and my son. My family stocked the cupboard full of food for me. They were all very supportive towards me.

At this point in my life, I felt good but I was still hurting inside. The dream focuses on the fact that I need to not worry about my son and I need to focus on myself and my recovery. It also tells me that if I do that, my son will be ok and that I will also be ok and everything will work out and I will have what I need.

> I then dreamt that I ran into Mary. We were talking. We even set up a date. She was with a weird guy that wasn't her type. I got the impression she was leaving him or coming out of that relationship. She was wearing brown suede shoes, but they were definitely not her style. The dream focused on her shoes. She had to leave to go to a party or something with this guy and she kept asking if they had alcohol.

I was concerned for Mary. Before we broke up she mentioned, on a few occasions, that there were things she wished she had done in her life that she never did. I knew that if I did not let her go and complete these things, or grow, that in the future, these things would rear their ugly heads and they would destroy our relationship. This most likely would have great consequences. Who knows, we could have been married and had kids by then. So, in her best interests, I had to break up with her because if I didn't, she would never be good to me or anyone for that matter. The dream is telling me that she did move on and was experiencing new things. However, these things she was experiencing may not be good. But, they were necessary for her to find what she did want and thus, important for her personal growth. Also, Mary and alcohol are things of my past that I needed to face and get over.

I had yet another dream:

> I was with another woman. I think it was Francine. We got back together and we were having sex, but before I could finish she would stop and start working on something. I would say, "Can't you stop working for five minutes?" She would say, "No!" Then, my glasses fell apart and I was running all over the house trying to find a repair kit to fix them. I then woke up.

This dream was telling me that Francine was very distracted by her own problems and was not able to focus on anything. It also tells that I have lost my "vision" and I was moving in all kinds of different directions looking for a way to "fix" my problem and get back on track.

3/09/04 This morning I dreamt about my friends Marty and Frankie. Our band was at an airport. Marty paid us all. Frankie and I got lots of money. My dad was there waiting for us at the restaurant. I had a lot of trouble gathering my markers and pens and sleeping bag. I had to have help. It took a long time because Dawn zipped my sleeping bag to hers and we had it out and I told her I did not want a relationship with her because I wanted someone my own age. This caused us to miss the truck that was to hold our luggage. I was pissed and started cussing about Dawn and women. This worker dressed in a white golden robe told me to be very careful about what I say. I made my way back to this room where Marty, Frankie and Jay were. We were up against the wall in this square area that was surrounded with wood beams. The square started moving. Then the floor started falling out from under me. We were supposed to grab a jeep and whoever touched it first got to keep it. It was a red Jeep Cherokee. I rolled over to Jay and he grabbed me before I fell through the hole. Frankie started to fall next. We could not help him, but he hung on and grabbed the jeep and put it in our box. Then Marty was there. Marty and Frankie then told this naked lady who was floating in the center of this room that the other people touched the jeep first when they were working on it. This guy in a white robe with gold trim walked up and tossed pebbles at each of our boxes then counted the ones that hit the other one and he counted with his finger, '4, 5, or 6." The naked lady, who was

> beautiful with long wavy brown hair, had a glass vase. She pulled out an eagle's head and out of its mouth a trail of glitter was coming and the girl said I could have him (meaning the eagle). "Kill him," she said. Then, Frankie looked at us and said we could have her killed if we say something to denounce the church. I ignored him and then Marty notified us we lost and we were out $1500. Both him and Frankie said, "Oh well" and I got pissed. Marty looked at me and smiled. He had a third eye in the middle of his forehead. I left and the dream ended.

This dream was telling me that the friends I had at this time were distracting me from what I needed to be doing (which was writing... the markers and pens). It also tells me, yet again, not to hitch my wagon to anyone else's (Dawn zipping her sleeping bad to mine) because it would only hold me back.

Furthermore, it discusses the fact that these acquaintances of mine had other, hidden, intentions that only benefitted themselves and that would end up costing me (the glass vase, eagle with glitter coming out of its mouth, the third eye in the middle of Marty's head). It also warns me not to worry about material things (the money) and not to give up on my beliefs (Frankie saying we could have her killed if I denounced the church). I needed to stay grounded and trust that as long as I am doing what I am supposed to be doing (teaching the world what I know), things will work out for me and I will be ok.

> 3/14/04 Last night I told God that I was very lonely and I wanted him to bring me that special person. I then dreamt that I was at a party at Mary's parent's house. Mary was there. We chatted and at one point we even held hands. I gave her a note and my phone number. Lorie from the bar was there too. Mary held my hand and said that she and I were best friends. I wanted to leave the party because it was getting late

and I needed to go home and get some sleep for work. Someone mentioned I had a dinner party while Mary was sitting next to me. They mentioned Lori was over and I quickly told Mary I had some friends over for dinner. Mary said she was probably out dating. There seemed to be some tension between us. Like we both wanted to just grab each other and hug and kiss, but we were both unsure if the other would want to or not. For some reason Mary had a bunch of freckles on her face and she gained weight.

The dream is discussing what I asked God for, a relationship, happening to me (the beginning of the dream). It also alludes me to the fact that Mary still needed to go through her phases and was continuing to do so, but I needed to move on from her (the second half of the dream).

3/30/04 Last night in my dream Francine, her friends and her mom Tony, were giving me a lot of grief over our baby. They gave me a lot of mental and physical abuse, but I kept fighting. Three of her friends were in a car with me. I said, "You have only got one side of the story." So, I told my side. One brunette, who was skinny, with long hair and a pony tail listened to me. She then laid down and cuddled with me. Then we were at a house full of people and she told me Francine would fight it (I told her that the lawyer was pushing me to fight her on a bunch of things I wasn't comfortable with). She then said the lawyer would file this injunction and that injunction. Just then an older Mexican ran in and said, "No, no, it's too soon." He ran out then back in and looked at me and said, "Just make sure you do what the lawyer tells you to do." I started to wake up and a bunch of black shadows were around me and people were working on me. They had a metal contraption in my mouth and side. It hurt, my spirit was fighting them and it all faded. I also saw a giant spider web in the hall way. When I came out of it all my side hurt in the same spot the metal contraption was touching me!

There were a lot of battles between Francine and I. She was a very cold person and had numerous mental issues herself, which needed to be dealt with. These would constantly resurface and cause problems in our relationship trying to take care of our son.

Before our son was even born there were indications that there were going to be problems, but I gave her the benefit of the doubt and just figured everybody has some sort of issues to deal with. So, I should just take it with a grain of salt. Boy that was a mistake!

Her and her mother used to yell at me for making the bed every morning and for putting the drain plug back in the shower so the cockroaches wouldn't come up through the drain. One night Francine, her mother, her stepfather, her brother and I went to dinner and some people sat down next to us blowing cigar smoke in our faces. Nobody would say anything to these very rude gentlemen, so I got up and moved to a different table so I would not have to breathe the smoke. Of course, I got accused of being hostile and nasty by Francine and her mother when all I did was simply remove myself from a situation that I did not like being in.

One time, when Francine and I were dating, she told me she thought she was still sane because every time she had a problem she ran away from it. This obviously, was red flag number one. Then, one night, we went out for pizza and she asked me what I liked on my pizza. When I told her, she said that she did not like those toppings. I told her that was fine and we could do half with what I wanted and half with what she wanted. She went ballistic in the store and insisted that we get what she wanted on the pizza. I finally said, "Ok, whatever is fine with me."

On yet another occasion, we were driving to dinner one night and there was this French restaurant in town. I read the name off of the sign and she went nuts again just because I did not pronounce it right. I thought, "Does that really matter? Is this tiny little mispronunciation worth getting that upset over?"

As you can imagine by the time our son was born the witch was on her broom! This includes her mother. Francine had a "C" section when our son was born, and of course, her mother went in the operating room with her, thereby not allowing me to do so. A while after our son was born, I was out in the waiting room patiently waiting to see him for the first time and the nurse came over to me to give me some information about taking care of the baby and to take me to be the first one to see him since I was the father. Francine's mother ran over to us immediately and ripped the information out of my hand and firmly stated that she should get that information and be the one to go into the infirmary first because she was the one with Francine in the operating room when our son was born.

There were several other incidents and battles throughout the beginning of my son's life. Such as, Francine refused to let me see my son in front of my lawyer in the lobby of the court room. She also tried to make me pay for everything including her mother for watching her own grandson. My attorney took care of that though. After she refused his request to let me see my son unsupervised she said, "I've got her now. That is exactly what I wanted her to say. I am good at this sort of thing and I will tear her apart in court."

Then, one day, Francine decided to take off to another state with my son, without telling me of course. They were gone two months before I ever heard from them and found out where they were and if my son was ok. I was going nuts for those two months. However, there was nothing that I could do about it now that she was gone because we did not have a court approved parenting plan and we were never actually legally married. Therefore, I had no rights in the eyes of the court and the law. I had made the mistake of actually trying to be an adult about the situation and get a parenting plan completed without having the attorneys involved in the process. I eventually got one completed, but it was after the fact that she took off to another state with our son. I went from being just 10 minutes away and seeing my son every weekend, to him being several states away and seeing him for a weekend every couple of months. Eventually, she would not let me see or talk to him at all. The only contact I have with him is through her. The only way I can do that, is to text her on my phone and hope she gives him the message.

Yes, I could get my attorney involved and rectify the situation. However, my son doesn't have the same feelings about his mother that I do. Therefore, by causing a lot of turmoil in order to solve the fact that I can't see him, it would only hurt him more and most likely cause him to dislike me. So, I remain idle and hope that someday, when he is older, he will seek me out on his own. Then we can talk and hopefully he will then be able to understand everything and we will be able to have a great relationship from that point on. I also remember my dream I had about when I went to a hospital and looked out the window and saw Francine and him together as a family unit and that I needed to let the situation go, so to speak so that everything would work out ok.

> 4/23/04 Last night I asked God to help me be able to date this girl Jenna. Then I had another dream about Mary. We met in front of someone's house and we ran up to each other and started kissing and we kept bumping teeth. She said it had been a while since she's kissed anyone. Then I grabbed some golf clubs from an old man who lived there. I took two sets, one was my grandfather's and the other set I thought was his but they were the old man's. I was supposed to meet Mary at my house. I put the clubs in my truck and woke up.

Here, I am being told that this relationship I was inquiring about would be fine in the beginning, but eventually it would not work out. I, however, had other things that I needed to be focused on.

> 4/26/04 Last night I asked God to help me with all of my problems. I dreamt Ron, the big boss where used to work, told me he knows I like to drink and smoke

pot and he was worried about my health and Tim, my old supervisor, told me how to get over those things. He said to get interested in something. He told me to play basketball, but… I am not tall enough. I woke up.

I then fell asleep again and dreamt I was back in the military and I was overseas and got shot in the left leg just above my knee. I got operated on and was on crutches back at the base trying to heal. I received the Millennium award and got promoted to Corporal. Some family took me in while I was healing. I hobbled everywhere on crutches.

This time, my dreams were warning me that my past will hinder me and that I need to let it go. They also foreshadowed the fact that I would eventually need a cane to walk and then end up in a wheelchair unable to walk, because of my health issues relative to my military service during the war. Only, I did not know that yet!

5/11/04 I dreamt that Mary was lying down on a couch or a bed and I asked her if I could hold her. I knew something was wrong. She said, "Yes, that was sweet." So, I did. She then told me while she was working on that dig with me over the summer she got an infected tooth from it and it turned green. I then woke up.

Mary did work for me on a dig one summer when I was an archaeologist serving on the board of a volunteer archaeological association. She also developed a tumor in her uterus some years later, which was removed a few months after we broke up.

5/27/04 I had two dreams. One, I was waiting for a bus. I had to pay for two tickets. The first bus did not show, so they comped me for the first ticket. I woke up.

In other words, I would have my chances. I was being warned not to miss them all.

In the second dream I was at an apartment complex working with some brunette on cashing out a cash register. We completed it. Then, later I had to complete it on my own. I did. I then went for a walk by the pool. High above, to the right was this big house with the wall being one big window overlooking the pool. The patio was huge. Everything was made out of cherry wood. I could see inside. It was nice and I saw stairs. Below were nice cupboards and shelves, all cherry wood.

6/10/04 I was in a kitchen. It was full of water. In the doorway to the dining room was a man without a shirt on and he had three earrings/hooks on his chest. I had to give him three swords. I gave them to him. He made me do it with the blades facing away from him. He hung them on his chest and guarded the doorway. We could not pass through until some sort of ceremony was over. Then, I was outside leaving. I walked by this car and its alarm went off. This blonde lady came out and she was checking every car. I ran and my flip flop fell off and I could not find it. There were other flip flops on the ground. She came up to me and touched me and said, "Tag, your it." She then started talking to me and I could not get rid of her. I then woke up.

6/25/04 I had two dreams. I was in a pool with Francine and her mom and I was holding my son. His pants had fallen down around his ankles and I said, "He looks like a little hoodlum kid." They said, "We wish you hadn't said that. If you want to keep having the right of seeing him you need to knock that off." They got all over my case and the more I said the worse it got.

In the second dream, we were in the court waiting room and the judge came out and sat next to us. They had a bunch of people and paper work with them. I had nothing. The judge said we should have a paternity test because that is what's best for the baby. I agreed and Francine just gave a fake smile to the judge and me and shook her head.

7/03/04 I dreamt that Mary and I were back together. We went out, kissed, had sex and were living together.

8/11/04 I dreamt I was in a war. We were in a battle, it was desert like. We ran into this building and Vietnamese soldiers came pouring in by the hundreds. We fought, but I got captured. They took me into a very dark room. I could not see. They sat me in a chair and hooked me up to electrical wires. I started screaming. They shoved rotten fish in my mouth. The soldier told me to shut up, it wasn't what I thought it was. They took the fish out of my mouth and untied me. He told me not to worry, it would be ok. Then we had a normal conversation and I woke up.

8/12/04 I dreamt this morning after calling in sick to work. I was sitting with Mary and she was wearing pink and her makeup was different. Her eyes seemed swollen. I told her that I really had missed her. She said the same, but not anymore. She said she guessed she was over it. I said ok and started to leave and this guy came up to me and said, "You have to try!" I said, "She just said she was over it." He said, "I know, don't worry about that. You have to really try!"

The main point of these dreams is that life changes and I really need to try and get over my past. Basically, I am chasing my tail. I am going from one tribulation to another without dealing with them. And, as I do that, things just compound and get worse. The dreams use things like "Mary" or "war" in them because these are things that meant a lot to me, were important to me, or that had a big influence on my life. Thus, I would remember the dream because those things would impact me mentally and leave a distinct impression on my subconscious.

8/20/04 I have a date with Frida and I also met a very attractive blond at a meeting yesterday. I had a dream last night. I asked God if I would be with Frida or the blonde. In the dream, I was putting a piece into a puzzle. It was the last piece of the puzzle. When I awoke I had the feeling of, "Don't worry, the final piece of the puzzle is being put into place!"

8/30/04 I dreamt that I was floating on my bed in front of a balcony Mary was on with a bunch of people. She did not notice me. Even after my attempts to get her attention. The bed started floating away and she finally saw me and waved and ran to the other people on the balcony to help her, but I kept floating away and I woke up.

9/02/04 Before I went to bed I asked God what to do about Frida, Michelle, or if neither one of them was who I was supposed to be with. And, if not, when will I meet the right one and what about Francine's child (our son)? I dreamt that I ran into Mary again somewhere. We talked about how mad she was at me and how she thought maybe the baby was part hers (*my ex was under the opinion that our son was just hers and she though she never had to let me see him*), like she helped make it. I then left. It was pointless. She just kept getting madder. I saw Dad in a courtyard. He was talking bad about her. He said, "She left a note to call her." But, he said that he didn't do anything. I told him to shut up and that she was a nice girl. Dad said, "Yeah right!" I was loading my guitar and amplifier into the bed of my truck and Mary came walking by with some burnout smoking a cigarette and kissing him. I said, "What the hell are you doing with that freak?" He said, "I am doing life in prison." I tried to talk her out of it. She said that he was taking care of her. She left with the guy's friend. She hands me the note dad had mentioned. She said, "Here, I guess I'll give you this."

People whistled at her. Then the felon stayed with me and talked about his motorcycle and then I woke up.

10/12/04 I dreamt that I was walking through a neighborhood. I passed a woman, who was blonde. She looked old in the face. She wore a pale green dress and an olive green shawl on her shoulders. Somehow, I ended up in the backyard of a house and couldn't find my way out. The blonde lady came out only now she was hot. She took me in the house and told me this was the only way out. She then started yelling at me for wearing an army jacket. I yelled back telling her I earned it. She started to get angrier so I ran out the front door (***Signifies my battles with Francine over how she thought I was crazy because of the war***). I found my truck in her driveway with the bed completely torn off of it. I looked at her and said, "What the hell did you do that for?" And I started running down the street. She chased me. People were coming out of their homes into the street warning me to stay away. It suddenly got cloudy and a tornado popped up. The blonde lady conjured it up. It was blowing me towards her as she screamed evilly. I was trying desperately to remember how to do the sign of the cross in Latin. But, I couldn't. All I could remember was sangre de Christo (blood of Christ), so I screamed that and she screamed in pain (***This section of my dream alludes to all the trouble Francine would cause me***). Then, I remembered the sign of the cross in Latin, "En nomen nobili, patri, fili, et spiritu santi." I said it and then I woke up.

10/13/04 All I remember of my dream last night is that I was in my house and it was raining and the house developed cracks and was leaking. Then, I went to my dad's house, it rained for three days. It seemed like it would never stop. His house developed a lot of cracks and began to really leak (*No matter where I go my problems will follow me and only get worse*).

10/14/04 I dreamt I was falling down through the sky and clouds with an old man who was wearing a white robe, had white hair, and a white beard. I said to him, "I have never felt so relaxed in my life." He said, "I bet you haven't." It was a bright blue sky with white clouds (*My future healing process and how great I would feel and bright my future would be*).

10/18/04 Last night I saw my old dog Sam in my dream. He was really skinny and sad. People were around and they said Sam had cancer. Sam and I communicated and we both cried.

I think that moment in the dream was about the very strong emotional bond between my dog and I (unconditional love). I actually learned what love was from my dog Sam. We were inseparable. Every time I came home from work he would make me get down on my knees and he would hug me just like a little human would. Every time Mary would come over and sit down on the couch next to me, Sam would scoot in between us and literally push Mary off of the couch and onto the floor. He was very protective of me and would not let anyone get near me. He was always there for me. This was something that I had yet to experience from a human being. No matter what, that dog loved me and I loved him. We had a bond that couldn't be broken. I have a new dog now. He is also my best friend. To this day, dogs are my favorite people! I have always had a special relationship with animals, especially the canine variety.

The next dream that I had was that I was looking for something I lost in this crowded restaurant. I was really getting frustrated because I could not find whatever it was. Then, I went up to this cash register and opened my wallet. It was so full of money that it fell out and on the floor. There was so much money that I could not even hold it all in my hands or pick it all up! I had to leave some money there. As I was walking out all of these people were getting on my case about being too cocky and told me to get the hell out of there. Then I woke up (***This dream discusses the fact of me being lost in life and eventually finding my way. Once I did, I would be very wealthy***).

1/04/05 I dreamt that my attorney called and said we had settlement papers but they were for a hearing in L.A. tonight. He then said, "What does she think, that I am stupid." I couldn't find a spot to park so I could hear him. I couldn't turn off the radio. I was trying to get into the college but I could only get into the hospital waiting room. Then, I had got into another room and couldn't get out. Someone tried to steal my back pack and walking stick that lay in the grass but I stopped them. I was in a class in which we received flash lights for emergencies. I had trouble shutting mine off and I couldn't find batteries. I was in a play in which I swooped down from the ceiling and landed on the stage at the end of the play.

1/10/05 Last night I dreamt that I was in Tim's bedroom. He and I were standing at the end of his bed and his wife was lying in it and she appeared to be sick. Tim wanted to help her so I offered to buy her a painting she liked and she said she would really like that. She appeared to be sad in the dream (***Today at work, Tim told me he was having some health problems and having trouble breathing***).

1/11/05 Last night I dreamt that I was in a tall cinder block building with two guys and someone who was blind was driving a crane and knocked it down. Then, I was in Vietnam on patrol by a river. I stepped in the river, following my platoon. They got back up on land and into the bushes. I saw the enemy and had to hide under the water next to the river bank. The enemy climbed over me and didn't know I was there. Then I was at a party at my friend's house from high school and Francine was there. She ignored me the whole time. Her mother was there in the beginning, but then was gone. My mom made fun of Francine and she heard it. She started to cry and came to me for a hug. I hugged her and she said thank you (***This is about my relationship with Francine. But, does it also suggest that she eventually would realize what she had done and apologize to me? I don't know yet***).

1/27/05 I had another dream that I was in a familiar place and could not find my way out, I dreamt about Mary, and some other girl that liked me who tried to pursue getting me to go out with her. Last night I also asked God for help with deciding to quit work and pursue something else. I dreamt I was dressed like a cowboy and I was cooking around a campfire and I was wearing sandals. The dram would focus on me dressed as a cowboy then on the sandals.

The dream is telling me that I want to change careers, but I have repressed it and have not done it. That is why it is coming out disguised as a cowboy with sandals. Also, being dressed as a cowboy and wearing sandals, signifies that I am doing several things at once and I am not sure who I really am or who I am supposed to be. I obviously need to figure this out and become what I am intended to be.

3/21/05 Last night I dreamt I was with Mary somewhere, like a park or something. She was holding my hand and I was lying down with my head in her lap. She was looking at my fingernails and we were talking. I told her I ran into her dad the other day and she knew exactly what store I ran into him in. It was like we were back together again.

3/22/05 I dreamt I worked at Home Depot with Frankie. While I was working one night, Mary came in. She saw me and went in a different direction. I told Frankie she ignored me and he said he'd talk to her. I walked off with another guy and I was explaining to him how we were going to get attacked tonight and we were walking back to the store from out in the desert. He said Mexicans offered Mary $270.00 to kiss her and he thought I'd offer her $360.00 to do it. Some lady was walking behind us and she said she'd take me.

3/24/05 Last night I dreamt that work knew I was going to quit so they let me go early on a Thursday, no party, no nothing. Everyone said goodbye in the hallway. Frida was crying and she wanted to give me a kiss, but couldn't cause everyone was there. I was looking forward to being out of there. I figured I would do landscaping for a while until I found something else.

5/07/05 This morning, I dreamt I took out my stepladder and extended it all the way up, but it wasn't tall enough to get to the top of the house. I needed to fix my leaking roof. So I pulled the ladder down and on the top, on each side of it, was ram's horns and they said Rhino on them. I took the ladder to a shorter side of the house. There were two men, and one was in a wheelchair, there to help me. Dad kept coming in and out of the house then I went to get a blue office chair on rollers like at work. A guy from Pure Fitness showed up and started an argument. He said he was working on his communication and he broke my chair. I got pissed and told him I was going to kick his butt. Then, eventually we started talking again about where we wanted to buy houses and I woke up.

7/25/05 I dreamt that I was on a side of a hill with Larry in military gear. The hill was covered in brush. We saw hundreds of enemy soldiers below attacking the hill. We climbed up to the top and ran into the house, grabbed some things and jumped in the truck to leave. We knew we were being overrun. I could not get my door shut because things kept getting in the way of the door. The alarm went off and woke me up.

In March of 2006, my book about my experiences in the first Gulf War, "*A Line in the Sand*," was published. (www.robertserocki.com) I had finally got the book published after six long years of writing. It felt good to get that story off of my chest and face it finally. It was the beginning to a long path I would end up taking towards recovery from the damage my past had caused me.

6/05/06 I woke up at 2am and I did not remember any dreams. I fell back asleep. I awoke again at 4:30am. I remembered this dream. My sister and I were in a van. We had the side door open and we were sleeping, like we were camping. I woke up (in the dream) and there was a bobcat right there. It was the same bobcat that I have actually had in my yard twice now. I panicked and scared it off into this neighborhood. I got out of the van with my 9mm pistol and my sister called animal control. They showed up. We were then back in the van a while and I had found out that my sister had gotten the bobcat back from animal control and she had it under some blankets. I said, "What the hell are you doing?" and she said, "Don't worry, they said it would be ok now." So, we then made it back to my parent's house. Everyone was in the family room, including Mary. I went and sat down next to her. We talked. She started yawning and said she had to go to sleep because she wakes up at 2am. I said, "I usually wake up then to." She said, "Instant message me" and I said, "Ok." The bobcat then came down stairs and left. A while later, I went back to the van and found the bobcat sleeping in one of the chairs under the blankets. So I left and then I woke up.

6/06/06 I awoke at 4:20am and I had dreamt that I was trying to catch a small fish by hand. I kept grabbing its tail, but it always got away. It hid in a crack and I still could not get it. I then woke up.

6/26/06 A few nights ago, I had a dream that there was a rack on a wall full of beer and caffeinated soda. I wanted both badly, but a voice kept telling me, "No!" So, I did not take any. The next morning I quit drinking caffeine. That was 6/20/06. Today is my first day without alcohol. What really made me stop alcohol was the dream I had last night. I asked God to make me a vehicle of his abundance, peace and happiness. The dream I had was that I woke up and went into the dining room and the front door was wide open with the morning light shining in. The, I woke up.

This dream has several symbols in it which all mean something to me, such as the beer and caffeinated drinks, the voice saying no, and the door open with the light shining in. This dream was telling me that I should "give up the past". In other words, let it go and move forward. Once I do that, the door would be "wide open" for me. I just need to take that step. God is waiting. It is all up to me.

11/06/06 I dreamt that Frida and I were in my house and it was very stormy outside and things were falling from the ceiling. I kept yelling at her to go back to bed because I needed peace and quiet so God could talk to me. I also dreamt that I woke up in bed and had several things in bed with me. One of the things I pulled out was my old football alarm clock that I had when I was a little kid. I then woke up.

This dream is telling me that in the future someone I love (Frida) will be with me when life gets stormy and things feel like they are falling down on me. Such as, me losing both my houses and everything I own and having to file bankruptcy only to end up suffering a nervous breakdown followed by a suicidal ideation eight months later.

This final event put me in the hospital for two weeks. Then, through numerous therapy sessions with a psychiatrist and a therapist, not to mention the five different kinds of medications they had me taking, I was getting better.

This all took place three years and four months after I had this dream. Peace, quiet, and God are what I would desperately need to make it through this foretold crisis. It is also telling me that I am taking too many things to bed with me that I need to let go of. Finally, the dream is telling me that I need to let go of my problems from my childhood (the football alarm clock was mine as a child). If not, I will suffer the impending doom the dream is warning me of.

> 11/08/06 This morning I had a dream that I was going to meet Francine somewhere in some town. A civil war broke out in the street and people started shooting at me and everyone else. I dove to the ground. There was rubble everywhere. I could see the bullets coming towards me and hitting the ground and bouncing, some just barely over my body, others, about five, hit me in my left hand. I finally got into a building to meet Francine and I showed her my hand and she kept getting her face very close to mine while I was talking. Then she kissed me. We talked for a while then for some reason her shirt fell off and her bra and breasts were exposed. I sat there. She grabbed her shirt to cover her breasts and we both looked over to my left and there was another man sitting there staring at her. I then woke up.

In this dream Francine, my ex, is representing the repressed emotions of anger I have towards her for leaving me in the night when I wasn't home and then, several months later, subsequently taking my son away from me and moving out of state so that I do not get to see him that often. There obviously is a war going on in the dream and it is really representing the conflict between my ex and myself. The rubble is symbolizing that things have completely fallen apart between us and that I have also repressed my feelings about that.

The left hand, which is commonly referred to as the bad hand, symbolizes the bad things that have happened to me and the bullets are the past, which was the war. The fact that I was hit five times symbolizes my son because he was about five at the time and that he was taken far away from me because my ex decided that I was crazy because of what I have gone through in the past.

Francine kissing me represents what I really wanted, which was a marriage and kids done the right way. That was one thing I always promised myself I would never screw up, but life happened. Francine's shirt popping off and showing her breasts symbolizes the fact that underneath, she is not who I thought she was. The man staring at her simply is denoting my repressed fear that she will meet another man and my son will forget about me.

> 11/14/06 Last night I had several dreams, waking after each at 2:30, 3:30, and 4:30. However, all I remember is that I wanted recognition for completing my first book. My mom and step dad and that side of the family were glad I did it, but that's all I got out of them. Then of course, my dad degraded everything I did and I got upset. After I did the thing that made me successful, we had a cake with nuts and it was overflowing with caramel syrup, which is my favorite.

This dream is about my repressed feelings of anger and sadness that resulted from the fact that I wrote and published a book and my parents would not even read it, which I wanted them to do desperately. I wanted them to know what I had been through and I wanted them to be proud of me for something since I felt like they never were. But, alas, the dream has a silver lining. It is basically telling me not to worry, that once I do the thing that will make me successful, my life will be overflowing with the things I like!

> 11/21/06 I dreamt that I ran into this girl Tony I had a crush on in grade school back in Detroit. She was working at a restaurant. My family went to a Hindu church and I did not want to go. Tony said she was married to some rich guy. I told her about me. Then a storm came and the back of the restaurant opened up and it was like night. Everyone went out to watch. Cars were flying through the air. It was then over. I told Tony I had to leave. She put her arm around me and squeezed and she said she had a little time and she would walk me out. I woke up.

I had such a huge crush on this girl Tony back in grade school. We were always together. That is part of what this dream is about. The Hindu church and me not wanting to go symbolizes the fact that at that time my parents forced me to go to a Catholic Church and Sunday school and I hated it. I even loathed it because of the fact that when I was supposed to go see my mother on my Easter break the priest decided to hold confession at that time and he told my father that if I did not do my confession I would have to start class all over again. I thought to myself, "Why the hell would God not want me to see my mother or not even understand I missed confession because of that. This seems rather contradictory to the word of God which is preached out of the bible at this church each and every Sunday."

Tony stating that she married a rich guy is about my feelings that as a child I thought we would grow up and always be together and get married. She was someone I cared deeply about and who, at that moment, cared about me and I needed that. My parents were divorced and I felt unloved except by Tony. But then things went horribly wrong when all the kids in junior high started constantly beating me up and calling me a wimp. My dad was yelling at me to fight back or he wouldn't let me in the house. I was afraid to go to school and I was afraid to go home. Tony quit talking to me even to the point where she never talked to me again. My one and only piece of happiness in my life now even hated me too. The end of the dream where we walk out together is another repressed feeling of what I really wanted all those years of junior high and high school. I wanted her to say she was sorry and realize that I wasn't the dorky wimp that everyone thought I was.

> 10/09/08 Last night I dreamt about the TV series Mash. I was crawling down the hall dragging something and saying something, but I was trying to be quiet about it. Then, I got caught by Colonel Henry Blake and I woke up.

All this dream really is saying is that I am still carrying things around inside me that are holding me back that I won't let go of. However, they will come out! After I had the Mash dream, I woke myself up yelling, "Shut up!" I just remember dreaming that someone was giving me a hard time, perhaps my dad, and I yelled shut up and woke up.

> 12/08/08 Last night I dreamt that I went back to work at the hamburger restaurant. I was still working at the museum during the day. Towards the end of the dream we got in trouble because of something we did like partying, etc.

In thinking about the dream this morning, I take it to mean that if I stick with the old ways, things will not work out. I must change, pay attention and continue down the new path that has been beset before me. It was after this dream that I did not have any more dreams like the ones I had over the last several years, at least not that I remembered.

CHAPTER 5

PHASE 4

At this point in my life, I was still living in the condo I bought in the desert, a new war was going on and the economy was going down the toilet and gas prices had risen so high that I could not afford to pay the gas bill, which was $500.00 a month.

So, I bought an historic home in the city closer to work and I decided that I would fix up the condo some more and sell it. Well, by that point the housing market had gotten downright ugly rather quickly. I then figured I better rent out the condo and try to ride out the storm.

However, I could only get someone to rent the house for part of what my mortgage payment was for. So, now I had a new house and I still had to pay $500.00 on the condo mortgage!

I had several safety and energy issues to take care of in the historic house in the city and I had gotten a series of home equity loans. I figured I would use those to fix up this house, ride out the storm and sell the condo. I could then re-finance the historic home when the market got better.

Well, things got even worse. When I found out I had lost over $200,000.00 in equity between the two houses, I knew I would never get that back and my attorney advised me to file bankruptcy.

The stress made my PTSD even worse and sent me into a nervous breakdown. I went to the hospital and found a psychiatrist to help me through these issues. I was out of work on the Family Medical Leave Act for 6 weeks. The doctor got me started on medication and it took about 6 months or so to get calmed down from the bankruptcy and losing everything I own to end up living in a 625 sq. ft. apartment with much less than what I had.

1/05/09 Just before waking I was dreaming that Tim and I were on a couch doing research, going through a pile of books. They were my books and they were about Latin and Greek literature and the Bible. In one of the books Tim was looking at the Stations of the Cross and their colors brown and yellow. The rest of the book was black and white. I picked up a book that showed a circular hole in the ground and I thought that was interesting as some sort of entrance. Then, the alarm went off and I woke up.

1/06/09 Just before I had to get up I was dreaming again. I was with a person soaring through the air. We went through beautiful country, pine trees, ocean, and mountains. Then we both shot high up into the sky and I came down in the water alone. I was with all of these people who were walking through the water like they were lost. We started walking and I met an older guy. He fell down in the water with rocks and sea weed. It was shallow. We all fell. We had to help the older guy. We knew we fell into a bad spot. We started to get up to keep moving and we found a bunch of fish. We kept walking and found our way back. The town, which I had never been to before had a big party for us in this restaurant. I was looking for the guy I was with that fell. He seemed to be the guest of honor. I found him and then went on my way. The place turned into a mall. I came across some escalators whose path was being reversed and speed increased, I couldn't go down. I ran into this family. My phone buzzed and I looked at it. It had automatically taken a picture of this family. Then I had realized the phone had recorded my whole journey, took all kinds of pictures. I thought, "Great, now I can write a book of this entire journey and become very wealthy!" The alarm went off and I woke up.

This dream spoke of my life and all of the ups and downs I experienced. It also discusses that it (my life) was all for a purpose. That purpose was to write about it so that the words can help people and teach them. Once I did that, I would become wealthy in all aspects of my life, not just with money!

1/09/09 I only remember part of my dream last night. I was sitting down at my computer at work typing up my canal data and Gary Allen came in for a meeting and sat down next to me. He saw what I was doing and started reading what I was writing. He said, "Hmm interesting, wow!" He was impressed with what I had written thus far.

1/24/09 Last night I dreamt that my family got in touch with me an invited me over to my grandparents' house for a holiday celebration. So, I went. When I got there everyone was up to their same old stuff, drinking and talking smack. My grandpa showed up with my Uncle. Grandpa was stumbling and said everyone has hangovers because they drank a lot the night before. My step dad was there talking like an idiot. I felt like I just did not fit in anymore, like I had changed and grew so much since I last saw them that I just did not belong there. So, I ate and took a nap, but they woke me up and were mean to me. So, I got fed up and left.

Of course they got mad about that, but I couldn't put up with their crap anymore. When I left I ran into Dr. Alrich and a friend of hers. So, we sat down to talk about what happened. Just then my mom shows up with a glass of wine in her hand and starts laying guilt trips on me. I got mad and told her off and said, "You will not manipulate me like that anymore!" So she left and her, my step dad, and half-sister were talking bad to me as they left. Then, Dr. Alrich sat down on the couch with me and said she was very proud of the way I handled my mother and that I did not fall into her trap. She then said, "Your mother likes to play a lot of political games and manipulate people, but you were very good and did not fall for it." Dr. Alrich was speaking to me in a very kind and gentle tone and she was all dressed up and even had makeup on, which I have never seen her with.

1/31/09 Last night I dreamt that the neighbor, Celeste was hiding under my bed with her boyfriend. She said they were scared to come out because I yelled at them. I said that's how I am, you have a party at 2:30am and wake everyone up, and I am going to get pissed. I then told them they could come out, and as long as they had respect for me, I would have it for them. Their cat came out and cuddled with me and then I woke up.

2/17/09 I had a dream, but all I can remember is that it dealt with four levels, but that's it.

3/10/09 I dreamt that I was in charge of an archaeological excavation that this contract firm I used to work for was doing. I had to inspect the burial site after they were done, then they had an end of field work party and they had beer, but I said I couldn't have any because I was a government employee and It wouldn't look good. We all became friends and I visited all of them in their dorm rooms. Two of the girls were lesbians and I saw them having sex pretty roughly, the veins on one of the girl's arms were popping out. Then one of the girls invited me along with everyone else, to her parent's house for thanksgiving. I went, but I was only able to find small plates and kept dropping my food. I had one glass of wine and someone showed me where the bottle was so I could have more, but I said, "I didn't want any more, I wanted red juice instead."

3/20/09 I dreamt that I was at the museum where I worked and they were having a party for an old volunteer and I was trying to look for a bowl big enough to put some food into but everything was too tiny. I saw Marissa she was very light colored, almost white and she was wearing white clothes. I then went out the back door and somehow ended up at my apartment. I was sleeping and these very tiny cats kept trying to get in the door, they were as small as my finger. Then I saw a tarantula that was on a cactus. The cactus closed up with the spider inside and the cactus rolled over and out came the spider and he crawled away. I then saw another spider crawling around but this one was smaller and webbed. I then went outside and I don't remember how, but a pony got out the door. I couldn't catch it, it was on the museum grounds and there were all of these horse people there. This girl offered to help me and she gave me a bridal so I carried her on my shoulders looking for the horse and we went into another building that was storage for dead reptiles and the girl said this is where the museum stores all of this stuff and we then went outside. I was tired of carrying her so I tried to put her down on the steps. I had her by her legs and her head hit the ground, she was very tall. Then we both lay on the stairs for a minute and Frida came along and saw us and she got mad and asked why I was carrying that girl around. I said she was helping me find the horse. She said but why do you have to carry her? Would you do that if it was a guy? I said she was just helping me, you're just jealous and you need to get over it. The girl walked away and then I woke up.

4/03/09 Last night I dreamt that I had to work at a Veteran's event and serve them and take care of them and listen to all of their war stories while they partied.

4/22/09 I dreamt that I was staying at this fancy hotel like place and a lot of the people I knew from Jr. High who picked on me were there. The people that owned the place were using us and hid all of our luggage and wouldn't let us leave. Patty from work was there and she got fed up and left. I kept trying to leave but I had to keep looking for my luggage. I finally had to leave it and forget about it if I truly wanted to escape.

This dream was the night before I was checked into the hospital, which is what this dream was foretelling. I had started drinking on this night because I was depressed again. I did not want to be at my job, I hated my life, and I was just in too much emotional pain to let this go on any further. So, I told Frida, "That was it. I was going to grab my shotgun and blow my head off. I can't take this anymore." She then said, "Do you want to go to the hospital instead?" and I said, "Yes."

At the hospital they took all of our possessions away obviously, even including shoe laces and the only place we were allowed to go besides the dorm and courtyard was the chow hall during meal times, but we had to be escorted. It almost felt like being in jail. I wanted to leave, but I knew I needed to stay. I knew that this was my opportunity to get rid of my "mental baggage" and leave it behind like in my dream from the night before.

After the intensive all day long therapy at the hospital for two weeks, I got to a point where I was ready to get out of the hospital. They had also gotten my medication straightened out and found out that I also had high blood pressure for which they gave me medication for.

Once I got out I was put into this Intensive Outpatient therapy that I had to go to three times a week for three hours each day. I was seeing my doctor once a month and a therapist once a month.

Since being in the hospital I have found my true passion and it is as Eckhart Tolle and Paulo Coelho say in their books, "When you follow your passion, the universe conspires to help you." My passion is writing and using my writing to help and benefit people who have their own personal struggles and show them that there is a purpose for it and they can get through it with a positive outcome.

Since I have found my passion, the true passion that lies within my heart, things have been working out for me in order to facilitate this endeavor. I was put on medical leave because of my PTSD from the first Gulf War and was able to use all of my sick and vacation time I had accumulated for money to pay the bills for two months while I was not working. Then, when I ran out of money, I got my tax return checks, which I had fortuitously filed late, and that carried me through for another month. When that ran out, I applied for disability through the City. As part of that they require you to apply for disability through Social Security, which I have done. It will be about five months before I hear back on that. I also applied for disability through the Veteran's Administration (VA) and they eventually determined that I was 30% disabled and I now receive a stipend from them as well.

While all of this was occurring I was writing. I was following my true passion. I had many bad days and weeks where I felt horrible and drained from hours of intensive therapy, however, I did my best t to stay focused on my mission and the present moment, which was for me to write. One of my therapists said, "If you have one foot in the past and one in the future what happens to today? You piss all over it!" In other words, all we have is right now and that is what we must focus on to be happy. That is also why I was having those three war dreams I wrote about in Chapter 1. That is why they were so vividly etched in my mind as a child. They were telling me the day would come that I would have to find the true passion of my heart and if I didn't, it would end up killing me. In other words, as Paulo Coelho said in his book, *The Alchemist*, "Find your heart and there will be your treasure!"

It is as if my life has been a play set onto a stage and I must learn my lines and perform them to my best in order to set an example to the people that inhabit the world. Especially, those who have not learned a thing and that are spiritually dead. We are stuck yet in another war and heading for a depression like the one in 1928. I also feel that we are headed for World War III if man does not change his evil ways.

And so, it is with these revelations that I head down the new path I must follow. The quote that was in the movie "Platoon" by Oliver Stone, now takes the stage of my mind, which it has done many times in the past. That quote was, "For those of us who make it we must rebuild again and teach the world what we know." It is with this poignant quote that I take my first steps down my new path and begin to teach you what I know.

My life seems a bit paradoxical to that of Benjamin Franklin's, the successes, failures, the love of reading and books, the mixture of conservative and liberal values, and the separation from our families.

This familiarity strikes me as quite odd and precipitates the question I have asked myself over and over again, "Do we really know who we are?" I asked my psychiatrist this question once, but I did not get an answer, just an analytical stare. Is there some sort of spiritual connection, if you will, between generations and individual man? Is the Bible right? Or, is science right? Or, yet even still, are they both right and interwoven just right in a perfect order?

Levi-Strauss discusses this interconnectedness in his book, "The Origin of Table Manners." On page 186, he shows a diagram (Fig. 16 The structural network of a system of mythic oppositions). On page 187, he goes on to say, "All the oppositions we have been dealing with since the beginning of this book can therefore be distributed at the points of intersection of a network with a discernable structure and which further analysis, incorporating other myths, could extend in new directions, while filling in gaps here and there. In the last resort, the differences that can be noted between the myths are to be explained by the levels at which the latter select the oppositions they use, and by the original way in which each myth folds the network back upon itself, horizontally, vertically or diagonally, in order to make certain pairs coincide and to reveal, in a certain perspective, the homology existing between several oppositions."

I once had a professor in college tell me that, "Myths are something the teller believes, but that no one else does." By this definition, the bible would be a myth. Let us now think about the implications of such within the framework just described by Levi-Strauss. In this way he gives "The Bible" structure, explanation of the differences within, and how, not only all the myths within the Bible, but the Bible, being a myth itself, is homologous to all other myths. Thereby, lending some truth to its suppositions, no matter how finite they may seem.

I have spent my whole life studying science and its empirical data and I see the logic behind its implications. I see where it is correct and amazing, yet I also see where it is wrong and possibly stretching the truth a bit when scientists become hyper analytical, especially when it comes to statistical analysis, which they commonly do.

I have also spent a great deal of my life learning about religion, when I was younger as a Catholic and when I was older being thrust into a war. Is there much more to our life than we really visualize? Is it that our minds are much to cluttered and blocked by our material pursuits and all the psychological baggage that we carry with us? If we would just let go, could this bring an inner peace and understanding that most of us do not know?

If we took time to quiet our minds and meditate, would more things not be revealed to us? Are we here to just get up in the morning, go to work, buy a house and raise a family? Does that not seem a bit simplistic for such complicated and scientifically marvelous beings that we are? There has to be more to life than the existence we have carved out for ourselves in I guess what we could call a "human experience." We must learn to find that inner voice or energy if you will, and listen to it. In Carl Jung's book, *Man and his Symbols*, he states, "A sense of wider meaning to one's existence is what raises a man beyond mere getting and spending. If he lacks this sense, he is lost and miserable. Had St. Paul been convinced that he was nothing more than a wandering weaver of carpets, he certainly would not have been the man he was. His real and meaningful life lay in the inner certainty that he was the messenger of the Lord."

I must also consider the people that I studied at work, the Hohokam. They excavated miles of canals to irrigate thousands of acres of farmland. And when I calculate current calculytic, hydraulic equations from latest books by the top engineers of our time, I find that these canals were almost perfectly excavated and the Hohokam flourished for over a thousand years living that way. Yet, they did not have these equations, calculators, computers, or the latest text books on engineering. However, they were able to do these things quite perfectly. How? This is a question that many archaeologists, including myself, try to answer. Again, we apply the latest and greatest theories and methods from the text books of the leading scholars in our field and yet, we do not really know for sure how the Hohokam did all these things so masterfully. We think we do, but how could we when we all ignore what is, in my opinion, the most important aspect of any culture, their spirituality. In other words, they had an understanding of spirit and their alignment with the energy that was within them and the universe and the interconnectedness of everything natural.

Archaeologists stay away from this subject like it's the plague. Perhaps, because there is no scientific theory or equation to prove that anything spiritual exists. There never will be, especially without belief. Native Americans are some of the most spiritual people I know. Yet, we ignore this very important part of their culture.

If we look back through our own history, we see that most of the successful people we know had some level of spirituality in their lives. And by successful, I do not mean something monetary.

If you are thinking that, then perhaps this book was a good choice for you. A person's success is not judged by what he or she has in their wallet. I think richness in one's life is judged by what he or she has learned through this life and how they applied what they have learned to the improvement and betterment of, not only their own lives, but also that of mankind. In fact one of our forefathers, Benjamin Franklin, stated that, "You cannot judge a man's worth by what he has in his wallet. You judge it by what he has contributed to mankind!"

If we look back through time to the beginnings of the church, we see a battle with the government for control of the people. Yet, we read things like our own constitution written hundreds of years after the beginnings of truly organized religion, and it implies that there is supposed to be a separation of church and state. Is there? Has there ever been? It's all about control and money. Look at all the churches that have been built through time. They are quite beautiful and truly expensive. I understand that they are supposed to be our affirmation of our love and dedication to God. However, God did not have money. He was poor by those societal standards. But, I find it highly ironic, that during the Middle Ages, the churches were rich and they had all the knowledge. The scholars were all clerics, which facilitated their desire to control the people. Now, there may be a separation of church and science, but the church is still money driven, just look in the collection pot!

If these churches are supposed to be such sacred and spiritual places proving our devotion to God, why are they the scenes of racial bigotry, horrible crimes against children, and foundations of hypocrisy? Why is the church always asking for money? Did God not warn us about greed? Jesus was poor, yet he had many followers!

Was not the basis of his spirituality being kind to one another? He did not require grand churches for worship or priests to speak to him on our behalf, as though there was some sort of spiritual hierarchy likened to that of our own government. Again, if we look back through time we see that people such as Jesus, St Francis of Assisi, Mother Theresa, and Gandhi, to name just a few, were spiritually revered, not for their churches, wealth and egalitarian rule, but for their kindness to fellow man and animals, a keen and intuitive understanding of nature, and how all of its forces work together in harmony and balance. They led by example and tried to teach us that this is the way our lives should be lived and not governed by a book of strict dogmatic rules that if broken, damn you to hell.

Hell is manifested here on Earth by us if we don't learn to change and grow in a positive way by treating one another kindly and respecting mother Earth. Really, we create our own Hell. We manifest it in our own world. It's not done by God or some evil spirit. It's created by us and should teach us that those ways are not right and hell won't go away until we change. However bad it may get, people still do not pay attention to these lessons. They are detached from what's really going on around them. They are swayed by people in authoritative positions claiming that it is they who know the way and lead us down a path deeper into self-inflicted Hell rooted in greed and power lust.

Our current religious beliefs are not really rooted in anything logical, they are instead forged by the social groups we impude ourselves into, whether they be secular or religious. Our religious practices are really ritualistic actions based on ambiguous symbols that we do not really understand. We think that by performing these rituals, like going to church on Sunday or saying five Our Fathers and five Hail Marys that God will see our devotion and take care of us and take care of our lives, even though we don't really understand what we are doing. We think he controls everything and things will work out according to his master plan, whatever that may be. This, however, really only reinforces the fact that we have lost our spirituality and our connection to the spiritual energy which is all around and within us all of the time to guide us, if we would just listen. In other words, God provides spiritual energy for all of us to "tap into." He relates it to each of our own specific lives. If we as people could tune into that energy, we would then learn the lessons we need to learn, and thus grow into, better and more complete human beings. Once that is achieved, then, and only then, do we achieve true harmony and really find heaven and the Garden of Eden.

However, most human beings are totally ignorant of this "spiritual energy" all around them. Thusly, perpetrating the maladies of, not only themselves, but mankind in general. Thereby, providing a petri dish of bacterium that precipitates the "devilish" cycle of paradox, which damns mankind to hell (earthly existence without tapping into spiritual energy) over and over again until this process is rectified.

For example, I will discuss some events that I experienced and quote some things that I have read in the words that follow so that you may have a more complete understanding of what I am saying.

My boss had gone out of town on vacation and left me in charge of the office. One of the things that I was left to take care of was a meeting between a large company and the local Native American Community. The communications company wanted to install some new wires and equipment to a cell tower on top of a mountain in town to improve communications of our police and fire personnel and the community. This mountain, however, was a spiritual location for the Native Americans. The company had its job to do and the Native Americans wanted the company to understand the spiritual importance of this place to them. It was my job to facilitate a mutual understanding between both cultures.

When the gentlemen arrived at my office, I explained to them what the Native Americans believe in and their perspective on life as I understood it. When they all arrived we sat down in the meeting room and began our discussion. I call your attention to the discourse the Native people gave. There were two of them, a man and a woman. The man was their spiritual leader. He stated that the mountain was extremely important to them because of the spiritual energy that inhabited it. He told them that there are spirits living in that mountain and the spirits are all around us all of the time. He then said, "in fact, they are here all around us right now in this room." The other native person that was there began to cry. The corporate men looked shocked; however, they understood the importance of the mountain to the Native people. The project got built and the company consulted with the tribe, and even brought them out to the mountain, to have them show everyone where to stay away from. I was completely moved by the depth of belief the Native Americans had in entities that no one else could see, let alone believe in.

Late on that night when I was sleeping I had a dream and in that dream that same Native medicine man visited me. From that day forward, nearly ten years ago, he would call me every six months or so and stay in touch. Sometimes, he even came to visit me and we would walk around the museum grounds and he would tell me spiritual stories about his ancestors, which he clearly believed were true. I think his belief was actually in the meaning behind the story and the story was created as a means to remember that meaning. These stories were handed down from generation to generation long before they had a written language.

I am also reminded of a story Dr. Wayne Dyer told about a dream a man once had about a butterfly. The dream was so real to him that he began to wonder if he was a human dreaming about a butterfly, or, a butterfly dreaming that he was human.

I have had many dreams like it myself. In fact, that was what the beginning of this book was all about. The three war dreams were all dreams that I have remembered, without writing them down for nearly 40 years. I remember every detail in spectacular clarity as if they happened yesterday. The three major stories I tell about the Revolutionary war, the Civil War, and Vietnam were dreams I had conveyed to me over and over again since the age of eight. The location where I was mortally wounded in all three dreams, the middle of my chest and back, still bother me today, especially when I am not doing what I am supposed to be doing. It is a reminder to me! In fact, I had those dreams continuously until I went to war in 1990 and lived through the experience, which is discussed in my book, "*A line in the Sand.*" (www.robertserocki.com).

I also had these dreams analyzed by my psychiatrist and, of course, it was quite analytical. She said I had those dreams because I was getting beat up at school and at home and it was like being in a war and it was killing me. She said that was what my brain was telling me. Although, there is some truth to the part about me getting beat up, I do not think it is as simple as this, especially since I started having the dreams before I was getting beat up.

To me, those dreams were what Eckhart Tolle describes as "National, Racial, and Collective pain bodies." They were trying to not only alert me of the pain I was going through as a child, but how that was also adding to the collective pain of the past. The dreams stopped after I had made it through the first Gulf War. They stopped because I had finally been beyond combat. I died in the dreams of the other three wars. This time, I lived through it. Now, I could continue down my path towards accomplishing what I am here to accomplish. This is explained in Paulo Coelho's book, *"Warrior of the Light."* On page 10 it states: "A warrior of the light knows that certain moments repeat themselves. He often finds himself faced by the same problems and situations, and seeing these difficult situations return, he grows depressed, thinking that he is incapable of making any progress in life. I have been through all of this before, he says to his heart. Yes, you have been through all this before, replies his heart. But you have never been beyond it. Then, the Warrior realizes that these repeated experiences have but one aim: to teach him what he does not want to learn,"

These collective pain bodies come from experiences the energy within you has had. It is an energy that is eternal. Your physical body may come and go as all things do in nature; however, the energy that perpetuates new growth is always there, always producing. It does not die.

There are numerous references to this in the Bible in Genesis. Such as, Adam lived 930 years, Seth lived 912 years, Enosh lived 905 years, Kenan lived 910 years, Mahalalel lived 895 years, Jared lived 962 years, and Enoch lived 365 years and he walked with God; then he was gone because God took him away.

We are not talking about physical bodies living all of these years. What the Bible is referring to is spiritual energy that lives in perpetuity. It inhabits physical bodies during its time here on earth. Once whatever needs to be learned and/or accomplished is completed, the spirit returns to God. In other words, it enters when the body is new and leaves when it is old only to move onto the new physical body until the lessons that particular energy are supposed to learn are realized and lived. Then, the cycle ceases. Once this evolution of the spirit happens, that is when heaven is found and that's where the energy, or spirit if you will, will stay. This is what I think the Bible is referring to when if refers to people living hundreds of years.

Based on what you have read in this book thus far, you may be thinking that I believe these dreams to be true, and I do. I also look at them as Dr. Wayne Dyer explains a person's life being split up into morning, afternoon, and evening. Those three events that I was in were the morning of my life. Those three experiences prepared me for what I have to do in the afternoon of my life. Write this book and teach the world what I know!

I must quote some things that I read Dr. Wayne Dyer's book, *"Inspiration Your Ultimate Calling,"* to give my beliefs some foundation. This particular verse comes from the Bhagavad-Gita, which is the Holy book of the Hindus that Gandhi based his life on.

> The self-dwells in the house of the body, which passes through childhood, youth, and old age. So passes the self at the time of death into another body. The wise know this truth and are not deceived by it. When the senses come in contact with sense objects they rise to feelings of heat and cold, pleasure and pain, which come and go. Accept them calmly, as do the wise.
>
> The wise who live from pleasure and pain, are worthy of immortality. Not pierced by arrows, nor burnt by fire, affected by neither water nor wind, the self is not a physical creature.
>
> Not wounded, not burnt, not wetted, not dried the self is ever and everywhere, immovable and everlasting.

> Some there are who have realized the self in all its wonder. Others can speak of it as wonderful. But there are many who do not understand even when they hear.
>
> Deathless is the self in every creature know this truth, and leave all sorrow behind.

I would also like to quote two more things from Dr. Dyer's book because they exemplify the depth from hence this philosophy comes:

> What is necessary to change a person is to change his awareness of himself
>
> Abraham Maslow

> You are a primary existence. You are a distinct portion of the essence of God, and contain a certain part of him in yourself. Why then are you ignorant of your noble birth? You carry a God about within you, poor wretch, and know nothing of it.
>
> Epictetus

People like to discuss how they are religious. Church is like a social meeting place where all the individuals therein have the same beliefs which were instilled in them through brain washing and trickery conveyed as particular religions. In fact Carl Jung, in his book, *Psychology and Religion*, states that religion is an observation of numinosum. "The numinosum is either a quality of a visible object or the influence of an invisible presence causing a peculiar alteration of consciousness." Jung even goes on to state later in the book that history has made us aware of the fact that biblical texts can be interpreted in many different ways.

Anyone who knows anything about foreign languages, would of course, also know this to be true because translating foreign languages, especially, Aramaic, Hebrew, and Greek, all of which the bible was translated from, is highly subject to interpretation.

Most people do not even understand what they are in church praying about and they are swearing an allegiance to a physical being that many people think walked among us. This person is really a physical symbol of what we all should realize about the spiritual energy that resides in all living creatures including the earth itself. Eckhart Tolle even mentions in his book, *The New Earth*, that the human brain has as many neurons as there are stars in our galaxy. Neurons, according to *Dictionary.com* are a specialized, impulse conducting cell that is the functional unit of the nervous system, consisting of the cell body and its processes. In other words, your neurons transmit energy! The energy that resides within every one of us!

However, most of us do not understand that. We have missed the boat so to speak. I think the best explanation of this is from a book I studied called, *Ritual Theory, Ritual Practice*, by Catherine Bell. It states, "When Abner Cohen addresses the ambiguity of symbols, he finds their multidimensionality to be essentially a bivocal structure addressing existential ends on the one hand and political ends on the other." Also, "They attempt to identify the ambiguity of ritual symbolism and deem such ambiguity to be essential to ritual."

Catherine Bell, goes on to explain what Phillip Converse demonstrated in a study of belief systems among elites as compared to those of the mass public. She states, "Among the public at large, beliefs and opinions become increasingly incoherent with each other as the level of sophistication and education decrease. That is to say, beliefs or attitudes are increasingly less constrained by logic on the one hand while becoming more affected by local group interests on the other. The dissociation of logically related ideas proceeds down the social ranks to such an extent that it is impossible to find any significant public participation in the belief systems found among elites."

She then goes on to say that the factor affecting the adjoining of beliefs was certainly the social affiliations of people rather than their psychological orientations. People do not even understand how they are being brainwashed and controlled by propaganda even when their own bible throws it in their face. A good example is the Catholic religion and how a person is basically deterred from taking communion if they are divorced or if they have become pregnant out of wedlock. The great Lucretius once said, "Tantum religio potuit suadere malorum (religion is able to persuade such horror)." A good example of what Lucretius said is happening now in this century. Countries are falling apart and thousands of people are dying because of uneducated interpretations of organized religions that are solidified by the people attending those functions and literally interpreting the dogma laid out in their religious doctrines and carrying them out through war.

A mythology should not be interpreted literally because it is a story full of physical symbols designed to facilitate the remembrance of it, which behind the symbols is conveyed an important spiritual meaning. We can obtain many good examples of mythologies which use physical symbols as vehicles to tell stories of spiritual importance from our Native American counterparts.

They were told this way before there was writing; hence they needed to have a way that would help them remember the stories so they could be passed on from generation to generation.

For example, the Hopi's who inhabit the four corners region of the American Southwest, have two symbols for Mother Earth. One is a square symbol and the other is round. The square symbol is supposed to remind us of our spiritual rebirth from one world to the next. It also reminds us of the way in which we come into the world through our mothers and how they cradle us and nurture us after birth.

The circular symbol reminds us of who give us life, our fathers (this is also attached to the sun, which without it nothing would grow i.e. energy!). And, it also symbolizes a plan for us by our creator and that if we follow it we are guaranteed rebirth. There also is a structural counterpart to this meaning behind the shapes, the Kiva, or, otherwise known as "Mother Earth."

The Hopis tell us of a multi-world universe and its physical changes using themselves as characters in a series of dramatic mythological stories designed so that they will not be forgotten.

The Pima, also of the American Southwest, have similar legends they tell in which they use symbols to enhance the memorization of these stories, especially by children. However, these stories have metamorphosed as their own history changed and the Pimans were introduced to the white man.

Bill King states it well in his introduction written in the book, *Pima Indian Legends*, by Anna Moore Shaw. He says, that these stories were told to Anna by her parents just as she told her own children, however, "but not in the same form. The inevitable changes that education, experience, and residence among non-Indians had on this Pima family were reflected in the manner in which the stories were told and in the ultimate forms that they assumed."

This makes me contemplate our own bible with its stories of creation through mythic symbolization. However, these stories stop with the crucifixion of Christ as if we have been dead since then and perhaps we have. Mr. King goes on to say how the Piman stories really began to change as they came in contact with whites and were subsequently translated into English and the "native cognate words and phrases sounded particularly out of place."

This also makes me ponder our bible and its translation from Aramaic, Hebrew, and Greek into English and how the front page of it says that it has been translated by over 100 different scholars from 11 different countries. Can you just imagine the ambiguity created by that amalgamation! Could perhaps there be a chance that something has been lost, diluted, and/or changed over time throughout these translations without us even knowing, all because of our literal translation of God's creation and our own? It's these slight changes from translation to translation throughout time that make me consider the fact that our own bible may be much farther from the truth than we really know.

We need to consider our own history and the evolution of governments controlling people and those people rebelling to that, and we look at the evolution of organized religion and its dogmatic prose, vying for control of the people and how they rebelled to that. Now we have leaders who run our governments and declare they are men of God, combining forces if you will.

Is there not some other lesson that we should be learning? A lesson that will not come from the literal translation of religious texts, but more from the understanding behind the stories meaning and how the symbols in those stories work to create that. Such as what C.G. Jung says in his book, *Psychology and Religion*. He states that, "The idea of those old philosophers was that God manifested himself first in the creation of the four elements. They were symbolized by the four partitions of the circle. The division into four, the synthesis of the four, the miraculous apparition of the four colors and the four stages of the work are constant preoccupations of the old philosophers. The four symbolizes the parts, qualities and aspects of the one."

In other words, Mother Earth is made up of four parts, earth (or the female body), wind, fire, and water, which are all the elements that form the natural world. Mother Earth and her four parts (earth, wind, fire, water), created God. God then created man with these same four parts. Thus, God is within man as much as God and man are a part of Mother Earth. Therefore since God is in all things of nature, which he created us with, we then are one in the same with God; God is within us as a sum of our four parts, just as he also is the sum of the four parts of Mother Earth.

Jung goes on to say that this symbol is found everywhere and throughout all ages. He even mentions the great importance the number four has with our Native American counterparts. He then states, "Although the four is an age-old, presumably historic symbol, always associated with the idea of a world creating deity, it is, however-curiously enough-rarely understood as such by those modern people to whom it occurs."

The Native people constantly tell us that we will truly never understand because we always must literally translate everything and it does not work that way. The Natives wonder why we study their culture and ways, profess to understand them, yet know nothing of our own creation and who we really are. I now am beginning to understand the wisdom behind these statements. I must also consider the fact that now, after European contact, there is a gap between the older traditional Natives and their younger counterparts. The stories and their meanings of who they really were are being lost. It is like we are literally watching the death of all of us right in front of our face, yet we do not see. It is like a battery that over time loses its energy and it is gone. We have to find a way to recharge if you will, such as the way we can recharge a battery.

Another good example is the Yaqui Indians of Sonora Mexico and Southern Arizona. Their stories are considered to be a form of entertaining history as Ruth Warner Giddings put it in her book, *Yaqui Myths and Legends*.

Their stories are now a blend of Native and Christian beliefs after their contact with the Mexicans. By blending the two, the Yaquis were able to retain their history as well as show their assimilation into Christianity. A lot of their stories tell of animals and in-animate objects that have great mythical powers and spiritual energies designed to be held within your memory.

However far-fetched these stories may seem to you; they reveal a deep understanding of spirit and the driving force behind us all. They also teach every individual to have great respect for the Earth and all of her creatures for they as well as the Earth, were sacredly created and we all are part of one another. In others, everyone and everything is connected in one form or another and one action affects all others. This interconnectedness affects all others. The interconnectedness can be spatial or temporal.

CHAPTER 6
THE BUTTERFLY

It is now that I return to my writing, 5/22/09, after somewhat of a hiatus do to my PTSD issues rearing their ugly head once more and another stint in the Veterans hospital. During the two weeks that I spent there I delved into my inner self and the complexity of issues therein. They mostly come from my childhood and the war of course. I was intrigued to learn that one set of circumstances had led me into another unhealthy set of circumstances and that this cycle repeats itself if there is no awareness of one's self. My first glimpse of my inner self poked through and made me aware that this behavior was not right and that it was leading me down a path I really did not wish to take. It is now that I write about what has transpired since my first stay in the hospital over a year ago.

Since that point I have realized that my six year relationship I was currently having with this woman was invalid for me in that she could not communicate with me and I needed more than that. It had been okay with me for the last six months because I was isolating myself and did not want to talk anyway. However, during my therapy in the hospital I was given an important word to learn and then put into practice. That word was, validate: to be honest with myself. It was with that word that I made my decision to split with this six year relationship I had with this woman and give myself some space and time to figure things out. I was changing so much that I was having a hard time comprehending what was going on and I could not handle the responsibilities that come with a relationship.

I was scared to death to ask her to move out because I was afraid of what her reaction might be and I did not want to hurt her, but I realized that I have no control over what she thinks or how she reacts and that is completely up to her. I only have control over my thoughts and actions. So, one evening I broke the news to her and I did not get the reaction I expected. Sure, she was a little upset and cried a bit, but she understood. She packed some things and moved back to her dad's house in order to give me my space that I needed to heal myself and continue my journey. We had plans to stay in touch, of course, because I did not know how this would turn out in the end.

Also, while I was in the hospital, I met a new friend Lucie. We shared a lot with each other about ourselves and because of the fact that we went through this experience of being in the hospital together a bond formed. It was strange to me in the sense that this bond is something that I have not felt since the bond that formed between me and my squad when I was in combat. It is interesting to contemplate the fact that shared traumatic experiences between people seem to form some sort of understanding between them.

Now, however, I have another decision that I will need to make over the next eight weeks I have off of work. That is to decide if I want to stay working at the museum and retire at 55 or just quit and go for it and try and make it as a writer the rest of my life enhancing people's lives with my books.

These decisions of change prove to be most difficult and scary, but alas, I have already made one such decision with my relationship and therefore, I have a foundation now from which to work. Money to live, retirement, all of those thoughts haunt my sole as I search my inner self for an answer. I know that I must not worry about these things, but I do. I guess I would much rather spend my life doing things that make me happy and enhance other people's lives than spending my life doing things because society says so. I think that all of us as humans would be much happier leading lives of doing things that make our hearts sing instead of doing things that crush our hearts and souls. It is ironic that we do this, especially in America where we are supposed to be free to do as we wish as long as it is within the boundaries of the law.

Yet, hardly any of us exercise that right with our own lives. We have fought, bled, and died for the right to be free and make choices, but we still cannot do it when it comes down to actually making the decision. Because, it is scary! We are afraid of what others might say or do. Who the hell cares? We only can control what we think and do, which leaves what we are worried about useless if we really think about it.

It really is not that complicated, but we make it that way. Why do we do this? Why do we so easily turn ourselves over to these lives we do not really want? It is the mass grouping of things and humans. It is everywhere. It is in our politics, religion, advertising, entertainment. It is everywhere and we allow it to strip us of our identity, of our inner-self which comprises our autonomy, something given to us by God to live our lives by. Yet we go to church, pray, meditate, swear our allegiance and love to him, yet we ignore the one greatest gift he has given to us, our inner-self.

I spent the last week or so reading Carl Jung's book, *The Undiscovered Self*. I found it to be quite interesting and enlightening. It was, shall I say, apropos for the world which we live in today. I even underlined several sentences throughout the book, which had significance for me.

> 5/25/09 I dreamt that I was at some sort of shopping mall with my Dad. I ran into Francine and even though I was down on my luck with my money situation she wanted me to give her an extra $50.00 a month. I couldn't afford it and I got an attorney,

she had one too and we went to battle over it. I don't remember what else happened.

    5/26/09 Last night I dreamt I was part of some sort of quire or musical group. We were to perform that night with instruments and I did not know how to play so I said something and the group said, "Don't worry, just do it anyway." Then we had a big pasta party and as I tried everyone's pasta, the further I dug into the bowls, the more things that were actually in the past were revealed, as if they were in layers. Then my uncles showed up, but I did not talk to them because they still had not apologized to me.

A while back, Lucie and I ended our friendship. It was way too much for me to handle. I was literally sick to my stomach with nerves. It seems at this time that I just cannot handle any sort of relationship with anyone while I go through all of these changes and repressed emotions. It is like after working on myself all day there is just nothing else left for me to give to anyone else and thus the relationship, no matter what capacity it is in, is too much for me to handle.

The next day at therapy I talked about killing someone in the war. Now I was really emotionally distraught. I went home and drank for two days straight and wanted to die again. However, after two days of emotional hell, I got better. This seems to be the pattern I go through every time I think or speak about the events of the past.

Lucie and I have decided to still be friends; however, we would only see each other once in a while. We would just talk on the phone mostly, for emotional support, while we both go through what we are going through. I was much more comfortable with this.

    6/4/09 Last night I dreamt that I got a call from a 214 area code on my cell phone. It was a message from Joe Stevenson, an old Marine buddy of mine, he said he was having fun with his son before he goes. I called the number back a few days later and his girlfriend answered the phone and said he had passed away. I collapsed on the floor crying about the fact that he was gone and I woke up.

Today, I went grocery shopping. I have recently been contemplating running a triathlon to help me deal with all of this negative emotional energy that is building up in me. As I was walking down the meat isle and I ran into Roseanne of all people. She was an assistant I hired at work about three or four years ago, she is a very pretty, tall, athletic woman and we got along quite well. We got to chatting and I asked her where she was working because when she quit the job I had hired her for she moved to Las Vegas. She said she was working for a local company now. She then told me she moved to Denver and her and her boyfriend broke up so she moved back here and she told me where she was living, which ended up being one block from where I was living.

She then told me she was training for a triathlon and I told her I wanted to do the same. I gave her my phone number and email address and said, "Maybe we could get together sometime if you want to?" She said, "Yeah especially since we live so close to each other."

I spent the rest of the day in a sort of shock about the whole event and that there was no way that running into her was just a coincidence. I was so moved by the experience that I even talked to my therapist about it the next day and she was equally amazed. She told me that that was no accident. It was a sign that I was on the right track and thinking properly on how to deal with my negative energy. I believe her and I am just absolutely fascinated with how the world works if we can only pay attention!

In therapy today, this woman was talking about an accident that happened to her over the weekend and how much blood she lost after hitting her head on a table and she kept talking about that over and over again. I started to panic because it reminded me of the war and all of the blood I saw. All of the emotions I had during those events came back, nausea, headache, racing heart, and shaking. I got up and left the room. The counselor made sure I was ok and let me sit by myself and collect myself for a while. She even brought me a glass of water. I returned to group a little while later, a little apprehensive, but better. I was so emotionally drained and physically soar when I got home that I literally crashed on the couch and fell asleep for an hour and a half. While I was asleep Lucie called, but I missed the call. I called her back and she said she would call later. She is pissed off about something, God only knows what now. I will see when she calls back alter.

I have an acquaintance who lives in the country of Qatar that I recently got in touch with. She is an emotional tornado. She says she wants to be friends yet she won't call me back or return my emails. So, I sent her an email about it and she totally reamed me out over it. So, I sent her one back telling her she was completely wrong and inappropriate and I am sorry that I bothered her. We will see what happens with that. She is just always so emotionally out of control. I cannot handle that.

I am still contemplating moving to San Clemente, California and getting an apartment, apart time job, and work on writing another book. My therapist said I could even get a little motor home or pop up trailer and live in one of those. So there are a couple of options there. For health insurance I can always go to the Veterans Hospital and get coverage for free so I won't have to worry about that. I will need to figure out how I am going to handle child support, day care, and plane tickets for my son with only a part time job. That will require some research.

I just had a thought, the Native Americans used the serpent as a symbol on a lot of things like rock art, pottery, etc. I have an idea of what it may possibly mean. Every so often the snake sheds its skin (outer or physical self) but the inner energy (its being) lives on and this symbolizes the fact that all physical things are fleeting and impermanent and it's your inner-self (or being) that is eternal. Rattlesnakes may shed their skin one to four times a year. Each shedding event adds a section to its rattle.

It is part of the natural cycle of things It can be seen in all of nature and this is what the Natives were paying attention to when they used these things as symbols, or reminders of "Being".

I am sitting here alone today as I write these things. I am truly alone and angry. My friend Lucie, well I thought she was a friend, gave up on our friendship so easily. So did Frida. She did not even put up a fight about leaving. You would think after 39 years of being treated like this and given up on, I would be used to it by now. But, alas, I am not. It hurts just as much as it did the first time.

I hurt yet no one seems to care. They are more concerned with themselves and nothing else. It seems the only way to get through the day is to drink. I sit alone trapped in my own madness. I wish someone was here, yet I pray to be left alone. The dualities of life and man haunt me. I pray for a break from the pain and madness, however, I never seem to get what I wish for. It seems that now a days the only way to get people to take you seriously is to tell them you are going to kill yourself. Then they can call an ambulance and get you to a hospital and feel noble about it even though it is as if they turned the other cheek on you to begin with.

Now I feel as if I will keep myself alive just to piss everyone off! I feel like I want to run away and live in the wilderness far, far away from people. I think people are one of God's worst inventions. Throughout my life I have always remarked that dogs are my favorite people.

I have many wounds from years of pain, yet none of them are physically visible. I carry them all within me. They are only visible to me, not that any person would care. I have fought many battles for myself and other people, yet I am taken by the irony that no one has ever fought for me. I used to cry, but I cannot anymore. The well is dry. I cannot access those emotions anymore. They are blocked from my mind. As I sit here eating sunflower seeds, drinking wine, and watching, *The Last Samurai*, I cannot help but wish someone would capture me and isolate me from the world as they did to Tom Cruz's character in the movie.

That is kind of what the hospital was like. I was isolated from the world behind locked doors, all the outside walls were tall with fences on top so that no glimpse of the outside world can get in and you can't get out. We slept on rubber beds with rubber pillows so we would sweat out any poison in our bodies, yet they kept you full of pills to make you feel better. Now that I am out it is as if I never went. I am just taking more pills. I am sorry, but I must ask, "What the hell is life for, what is the point?" I suppose I may never know. Or, will I?

In the same movie I mentioned above, Tom Cruz's character just said, "Thank you, you have been very kind to me." He said this to a woman who took care of him. That would be nice to know what that feels like, but I guess I will never know. I surmise that in life everything has its time to come and go, but to have that feeling, just once, I will never know. It is as if I have been set to a life of suffering. For what, I do not know why.

Last night I started to feel better. I had decided that I needed to give myself a break. It is ok that I have relapsed. I have been through hell. But I am still moving forward and it is going to happen. I basically said to myself, "It is what it is." I made friends with my suffering so to speak. My doctors all told me that during the healing process I will have relapses and setbacks. It is all a normal part of the process. I just have to keep trying.

I did wake up feeling good today. I went to therapy and spilled my guts again and I talked about the awful reaction I get from people and how they all think I am this crazy killer because I am a Marine. I got a huge reaction, but one that was quite different than what I had expected. One older gentleman cried and told me how courageous a man I must be and he thanked me. He told me that all of his relatives were in Auschwitz during World War II and it was the Marines who came in and saved everyone. To this day, when I think about what he said, the hair on my arms stands up and I get goose bumps knowing I was part of the United States Marine Corps. An organization that has fought for and saved many people. Another girl also told me, "Thank you." She also mentioned how brave I am and to hell with the people who think the other way about me. She said, "You have to wonder about their mentality in the first place."

I got this reaction out of just about everyone and I felt good because for the first time, I felt true acceptance and gratitude for who I am and what I have done and it felt great! I also told the group that my psychiatrist told me that I also have a part in helping people understand Veterans. I may be afraid to talk because of the reaction I may get, but I also have an obligation to tell them what I am going through so they really know what it's like for us Veterans. It was a very profound statement and they agreed. So, I grew today. I left myself with two questions today, "Who the hell cares what people think? Does it really matter?"

Today my goal, after coffee of course, is to make a list of what I need to do this week in order to move to San Clemente, California. Then, I also need to look up and make a list of places for rent and jobs so I can see how I will be able to afford this. Frida came over yesterday and we talked about how we were both doing and we are going to go on a date Friday night. She said she would consider moving to San Clemente with me and that would be a big help. She is so nice. Hopefully, things work out for us. I do feel better about our relationship now that we have been apart for a while and I have had a chance to concentrate on my therapy and recovery.

It is 8:11am and I am sitting here thinking about the fact that I will run out of sick and vacation time in another week or so, which means I will then go on unpaid leave and the City will also make me start paying for my insurance. On top of that, my child support won't be getting paid, which means I would go to jail. I talked to the City about long term disability, but they said it won't get approved if my condition is military related. That's a nice thank you for defending my country. If it wasn't for people like me, the people wouldn't be free or have the freedom to choose the job that they want and that's the thanks I get!

So, now I am trying to deal with this the best I can without freaking out, but it's getting hard. I am going to try and read now. Last night I started to drink, only beer, but I stopped myself, listened to some nature songs and laid in bed and read about the Loretto Chapel in Santa Fe, New Mexico, which I have visited.

Then, I meditated and eventually fell asleep. So, I made it through the night. Now, I just have to make it through today somehow.

I must also remember to have faith. I am really going to try and work on this today; to have faith that everything will work out with my therapy, disability, and money situation so that I may continue this journey I have now begun. Having said that, I recall two paragraphs from the book I was reading last night on the Loretto Chapel. They are as follows: "Can anyone of the hundreds who admire its beauty today understand what it meant to those nuns to assist at the dedication of that chapel knowing that their faith more than their money went into its erection."

This inspires me to believe that as long as I am doing what I am supposed to i.e., therapy, reading, writing another book, that everything will be provided for me and worked out in such a way that I can accomplish that mission which has been placed before me to accomplish. And, if I veer off track, things will go wrong and, therefore, I should let that be a reminder to re-focus on what I need to be doing.

The second phrase from the same book is as follows: "I don't believe I would ever have known the blessings of peace had I not experienced the effects of war."

> 6/17/09 Last night I had this weird dream I was still interested in archaeology. I was going around checking out sites, burials, and spiritual sites especially. I was even finding them on my own. I wasn't working for anyone. I was just doing this all on my own. There was also this attractive blond lady, who kept trying to have sex with me, but we would never get to finish, we always got interrupted somehow. In the dream I met her through the archaeology stuff I was doing.
>
> 6/18/09 Last night I dreamt I was back in the war. I constantly kept losing my rifle and they would only give me a pistol and I kept screwing up. I went on a mission where I was surrounded by the enemy inside an area that was fenced in by barbed wire. I only had

a pistol. So, I shot at each one of them but the bullet would come out in slow motion and hit them but it would not stop them. I felt intense fear and panic like I felt in the war.

6/19/09 In the dream I had last night I was at my dad's house, but my step dad and mom lived there and my step dad was sitting out on the balcony in the cold. I was in my dad's room in my underwear looking at him. They were all going out with some people and they had a baby sitter come over. I kept trying to get my shorts from my step dad so I could put them on because the baby sitter was there. I had a hell of a time getting my shorts and getting them on. I was very frustrated. Then, I found out the baby sitters were two people from work that really irritate me and of course it did. The rest of the dream involved me in the kitchen trying to shut the fridge to keep the dogs out of there because they were eating the food, which also frustrated me.

The last two nights I have gone out with Frida and both nights I got drunk. This bothers me and It also bothers me that for the past two weeks I have been drinking, not getting drunk, but having a couple of beers each night. At first, I was ok with this because I used to drink a lot and hard stuff like Scotch and Vodka. So, since I am only having beer and occasionally wine and not getting drunk like I used to, I was viewing it as a victory, as progress so to speak, because it was less than what I used to do. However, now, especially after getting drunk the last two nights, I am beating myself up over it. As I am writing this I am sitting here trying to observe how I am feeling because I know I shouldn't be beating myself up over this. It is what it is. It is over and done with; it is in the past now. I am feeling this nervous tension and anger towards myself right now. I am letting myself feel these emotions. However, today is a new day and I have all new choices to make. It's like a "do-over" I think.

I need to do something about this drinking all the time because I want to be pure and I need to think about why I am still doing it even at a diminished level. Perhaps subconsciously I am still feeling guilty about my life and the war and I am still trying to numb those feelings so that I don't have to experience them. Because up to this point, that's all I knew how to do. But, just maybe, it is an old habit that is fading!

I have changed a lot and made a lot of progress, but it may just be as simple as this being one more layer of the onion that I must peel away. Just be as simple as this being I have to remember baby steps. One issue at a time and all things take effort and time to accomplish. I am going to contemplate this today. I have been doing pretty well with dealing with my other emotions in other ways than I used to by observing them and channeling them into something healthier or better for me. I now need to learn to do that with the drinking. I need to pay attention to what I am feeling at the moment I decide to drink, feel it, and then channel it into something else more productive, or should I say, more nurturing to myself.

I have also had this strong attraction to Muslim women, which certainly perplexes me since I went to war in that part of the world. I do not know why I am so attracted to them, or should I say so compassionate toward them. The only thing that I can think of that would contribute to such an emotion towards a specific race of people in my life is that it quite possibly has its roots in the first Gulf War that I was in and saw how horribly the women were treated there when we liberated Kuwait City from the Iraqi's. Or, it is from the time we were driving through the desert and we saw a woman with her family without a veil on and we honked and yelled at her and her husband subsequently beat the hell out of her for allowing herself to be seen with her face uncovered by another man, especially white ones.

The compassion that I feel so strongly must be coming from the guilt I feel subconsciously for doing what we did to that poor woman. In fact, as I am writing this I am noticing these horrid feelings building up inside myself, like I want to punish myself for being so bad. However, I am deciding to let myself feel this way for a while and observe it so that I may let these trapped feelings out.

At one point in my life this compassion or attachment was so strong that I almost ruined my relationship with Frida because I got so emotionally involved with a Persian woman. It was like I could not control it when I was around her.

I must say, after allowing myself to feel the emotions that had come over me earlier this morning it lessened the amount of time I felt that way. While I was allowing things to be as they are, I began to organize my medications in my pill box. The next thing you know, I had completely forgotten that I was feeling all of this guilt and shame for what I had done to that woman in the Saudi Desert and I had realized that I had moved on from it.

I have been beating myself up all day because I got depressed about the impending Father's day holiday and I got drunk and stayed up all night. At least I was working on a song that I am writing. I have not done anything all day accept be depressed. I wrote an email to the Persian girl telling her how I felt about her. I seem to still have a hard time getting her out of my head.

I need to stop this drinking shit. I want to stop punishing myself this way. Or, should I say using it to numb my pain. I was doing so well with it after I got out of the hospital, but now I seem to be reverting to my old ways. I have just got to stop. I keep saying that, but I do not do it. I guess I don't want to quit yet. When will enough be enough? I am really getting mad at myself for this right now.

I am still really depressed and feeling bad today. I wonder if it is just the onslaught of emotion coming out after my realization Friday about Muslim women. This usually does happen to me. Once I get something off of my chest I go through this emotional dumping, if you will, and I become completely depressed, feel like crap and get soar for two or three days like someone beat me up. Plus, on top of that, I am bummed about Father's day. I just have to keep trying and move through it. It is very hard, like being in combat, like I am in this constant battle. However, I have to keep trying. I have come too far to give up now.

6/22/09, 2:00pm. I am sitting here at a restaurant ordering lunch and had the urge to write. I got a pen from the waitress and started writing on napkins. I wrote about my day today. The waitress thought it was cute and brought me a pile of napkins to write on. So, for today they are my journal and I wrote as follows: "So, today at therapy, I talked about my so called enlightenment from Friday when I realized why I had this affinity for Muslim women. It turns out it is not just an affinity but compassion and love because of what we did overseas. This was determined by the group and the group counselor. They had a lot of kind words and support for me. They talked about my first book, *A line in the Sand*, and all of the horrible things I went through in the war and what a brave and courageous man I am to have gone through all of that and then have the strength to face it, relive it again, in front of everyone, in therapy to try and get better.

They also told me I am beating myself up much too hard over everything. That much I do know and I think it's our inherent nature as human beings to have to punish ourselves for things we do. It is like our mind feeds off of this negativity and anxiety and craves it. It is such a draining battle to fight and face. Now I know why veterans spend their lives drinking and doing drugs just to numb themselves until they die and make it out of here. Just like when I was in the war and we spent our days searching for some sort of escape from the pain and ugliness and prayed for the day we would get the hell out of there. It's a cycle, isn't it? A vicious one at that, no doubt. We were to return home with the choice of wasting our lives in a bottle of booze, killing time until death bequeathed us, or face it and relive the war again and again, over and over. Where the hell do you find the strength to do that?

Give me the bottle! No, I can't. Come on face it. You can do this! No, I can't. Awe God, or someone please help me! Can't this day be over? Hell, it is still daylight. What do I do now?

So, as I was sitting here thinking of my day, as irony would have it, I started talking to this waitress. It was a waitress who had waited on me once before, but she did not remember me. Come to find out that her roommate's boyfriend is a Marine who just got home from Iraq and we began to talk. She had a bit of trouble with a DUI, but we had some things in common. The conversation went smoothly and felt quite natural.

Interesting, I might say. I did not expect this to happen. Especially in a restaurant. I am amazed at life and how perfectly ordered it can be. Everything has its place, its time, and its purpose. Who does all of this ordering of things? Who puts everything in its perfect place at its perfect time, in perfect harmony? It is truly amazing when you think about it.

At times we are small and insignificant, yet at other times the world seems to revolve around us at one precious moment in time. How in the Hell does this happen? Who manages this? This person or thing, whatever it is, has incredible skill and a lot of compassion for us.

> 6/24/09 4:27pm Well, yesterday, after the day I had on Monday, I woke up with a hangover from the night before. The emotional tumult that I was going through was just too much for me to handle. A lot of stuff came out in therapy on Monday. On Tuesday morning I still felt the emotional drain. I was sore and tired on top of the hangover. I felt so awful. A lot of guilt and shame was still coming out and I found that all I could do all day was lay in bed and drink more beer to get through the day. All I kept hearing was Steven's voice from therapy telling me, "Quit beating yourself up. Give yourself a break, you have been through hell man!"

By the time evening had rolled around and I had finished a six pack, I quit drinking as somehow I felt punished enough and at the same time the flood of horrible emotions had stopped. I ate dinner, drank a bunch of water and went to bed and read for a few hours.

I was still very tired this morning, but I managed to get up and get myself ready to go to therapy. I did not say much today because I felt as if I was still recovering from the emotional bombardment of the last two days I was still so tired that this afternoon I laid down in bed and took a two hour nap.

    5:30pm I really need to work on quitting beating myself up all of the time. I have not meditated in a while. I need to get back to a schedule during the day. I should get up at 5am and go run a few miles. Then come back and go about my day and plan it. Even to the extent where I plan not to drink. Social things are ok once in a while, but when I release a lot of emotions from the war I tend to drink and punish myself because they are so awful and powerful, but I have to keep releasing the pain and find a healthier way to deal with it.

    Living alone doesn't help, but those are the circumstances I face. Tomorrow is another day and another chance. I did well today. No drinks at all. So let's see if we can do it again tomorrow. I have therapy in the morning so hopefully that goes well. I need to do a schedule tomorrow morning. I want to get up at 5am, run and then plan my day.

    6/25/09 This morning I got up a little after 5am and went running, came home and meditated because it was peaceful, then I took a shower. I then read some pages out of Eckhart Tolle's book, *New Earth*, and they really made me think about this past year. It made me think about how I have lost both my houses, filed bankruptcy, been mentally ill on the verge of suicide, spent two weeks in a hospital, and nearly the entire year previous to that in therapy, which I still continue to go to. I thought about how Frida and I got an apartment and now she no longer lives here and all of the stress this has caused and brought back my PTSD on top of that. It's like my life is changing and things are being cleared out of the way for new things to enter, for a new life, a new purpose. The therapy is helping me to clear things out of my head like dead branches out of a tree so that I may flourish and have a clear mind to look at things and observe them as they come into my life. As every step I take is a new one down a new path leading me to a new destination? I don't know where that is, but I have to trust that it's where I am supposed to be and things will work out for the best for me and my new purpose, which I think is to be a writer and teach the world what I know.

I can't go back to my job. It is bad for me and takes away all of the energy and time I need to write. I don't know how I am going to make it or what's going to happen, but I know I have to go down this new path and trust that things will work out for me in their proper time and place. I don't even have an idea of how I will make money or survive. I can't worry about that. I have to do what I must do knowing that I will be provided for. This is hard to do, but I seem so compelled to do it. It's scary to think about it. It's scary to do it and it most certainly is scary to think it's actually all going to work out!

6/26/09 I have been sleeping all day because I got drunk last night. I had a very angry dream where I was angry at my dad, my mom, and my sister. I was so angry that I bit down on something in the dream and busted all of my teeth out and throughout the dream. I kept spitting pieces of my teeth out until I spit out a necklace that I bit down on that originally broke my teeth. I kept yelling at everyone, mom, dad, Lori throughout the whole dream about all the messed up things they did to me. They were trying to look something up in the phonebook because they thought I was an alcoholic but only drank because of them. While they were doing that I heard dad say, "Well you know how your brother is. I couldn't get him to do anything when he was younger until I pissed him off." Then I said, "Yeah and that's half the reason why I am messed up today!" Then I woke up.

9:43am I have had enough of this anger and sadness that I carry with me from my family. It's really been eating away at me since I had that dream last night. I have decided that I am going to write down all of my anger to each one of them in a letter then forgive them and move on today. I am not going to send it to them because that will only start World War III and my intention is to get this off of my chest and writing it all out, I think, will accomplish that. So, I did it and it did help.

> 6/28/09 Last night I had a dream I was on a trip with a bunch of people including a beautiful dark skinned woman. We had to get down this cliff to the boats and we had to slide straight down the cliffs, sometimes falling a distance. We landed in the water. Everyone was swimming towards these boats that were there to pick us up. However, there was not enough room for the dark skinned girl and me and we had to swim. Tiny sharks were attacking me but we were able to talk and get to know each other. We finally made it to an area that had a pier and we got onto land. We stayed in this place for a while and got to know each other, then we finally found a boat and got on it and sailed away together and I woke up.

6:05pm Now that I have released these tumultuous feelings and fiendish people from my life I may move on and fulfill my purpose. It feels as if I was a tree full of dead branches that have been trimmed away so now you can see the few in the middle that are still alive. Now these branches will be able to flourish and grow into a beautiful tree to shade all of mankind, to house the animals, to provide food for them both. It is with these feelings that I now take my next step forward without the weight of a world on my chest. Yes, now I am free!

> 7/03/09 12:51pm Last night, due to the impending fourth of July holiday of course, I went and bought

some beer expecting to go through my same normal procedure that I go through every veterans related holiday. I usually get depressed, drink, cry, and emotionally fall apart for two or three days. So as I sat there and drank watching veteran's movies I noticed that nothing was happening to me. I figured it must be because I wasn't drunk enough yet. So, I drank some more, but nothing happened. No crying, no emotional breakdowns, no deep sadness. It was as if it was just memories to me, nothing more. There was no emotional charge attached to those memories. In fact, it was so strange that I didn't know what to do with myself because I had been living the other way for so long. This therapy stuff is really working. I am getting better and I have to admit that I do feel more at peace. So much so, that I sent Francine a text message that I was sorry for the past, that I loved her as a human being, and that at the very least I hoped we could be friends. She sent a text back saying, "Thank you, it means a lot to me." I was stunned. It's only 1pm and I have already had such a profound day.

7/06/09 4:14pm Well, after what I thought was going to be a bad holiday, did not turn out so bad at all. I thought it was going to be bad because Friday evening Frida told me she needed space from me (even though she doesn't live with me anymore) and she does not want to talk to me. She said she should have broken up with me after the Sakeen incident almost two years ago. I said ok, but when I got off of the phone I was devastated. How could she do such a thing on a holiday weekend that she knows I would have a hard time with and need someone to talk too.

Well, I felt so bad and so alone sitting in my chair on the patio, I was stunned. I sat in that chair drank, and watched people come and go all evening Friday, all the way through Saturday morning.

Still sitting in my chair I watched the sun come up and then I thought, you stupid idiot. Just call Frida and ask her to talk to you. Maybe she just needs to hear me ask her to call me even though she said she did not want to talk to find out what kind of feelings I had for her. So, I sent her a text message and she called me back and I explained to her that I was hurt and she said she just felt like she had to get that off of her chest from the Sakeen incident and she was hurt about that. So, she ended up coming over and we went to dinner and had a nice evening together. I felt relieved. Because of this incident I realized how much I really do love her and how much of a friend she is to me.

    She came back on Sunday evening with some groceries for me and we had a fancy dinner together with a very nice bottle of wine. We discussed our relationship and her moving back in. She said that her sister Linda is moving out with her boyfriend at the end of the month to a new apartment and she did not want to leave her dad by himself and said I could move into their house and the three of us could live together.

    She and her dad's name are on the house. She said I could work on my writing and fix up the house and we wouldn't have any rent to pay, just groceries and my child support and daycare. It sounds like a good idea to me. It is right in line with what I truly want to do and it's a situation that everybody in it wins. We also talked about my continued health care and need for insurance.

    We discussed it and for one, I could go to the VA, or two, we could get married and I could get on her City insurance and have the same coverage I have now. I would just have to get her switched to Blue Cross Blue Shield like I have and I could keep all of my same doctors. So, we will definitely need to talk about this some more as it seems to be a good solution for everyone.

> 7/07/09 I talked to the doctor yesterday and she seemed to think me hearing noises and seeing things was brought on by the fourth of July Holiday and me thinking about the war so much. She also had me talk about things in the war that bothered me like killing a

person, watching my own people get blown to pieces, seeing thousands of pieces of body parts in the Iraqi bunkers and strewn about the "Highway of Death" into Kuwait City. She made me talk about things I was ashamed of doing like killing rats with my bayonette and a shovel like they were the enemy and then parading them around like trophies. At the end of our session she said I should go give myself a reward for all of the hard work I have been doing on myself. I left there feeling disconnected, shaky, fuzzy and numb, but decided to follow the doctor's advice. I bought a six pack of beer and went home. I turned on the Detroit Tigers baseball game. I put my ball cap on, got out m y glove, and my baseball from a Detroit Tigers game when I was five. Mark Fidrich was pitching and Norm Cash hit the ball into the stands and my dad caught it. So I loaded my mouth with sunflower seeds, had a beer, played catch with myself and watched the ballgame. This was my reward and I decided I liked it and watched the whole game that way.

I got my insurance and rent paid. Frida stopped by with two checks for me. It's funny how things work out when you listen to your inner self and do what you're supposed to be doing. When I paid the rent today they even charged my $25.00 less than what they were supposed to!

I have also been thinking about this idea of me moving in with Frida and her dad that she posed to me. I feel like I need to listen to my inner voice and retain my space while I work on myself and my book, like I still want to see her every few days, like I need her friendship and help, but I also feel like I need to leave things be and see how they unfold. I feel as though things have been cleaned out of my life to make room for something else and that will come with time as long as I listen and don't mess with the natural order of things. I need to tell her all of these things and I am scared how she will react, but I have to do this and be honest with her. I just hope she doesn't break off our friendship because I do love her very much and like I said earlier I need her help and friendship. I guess to sum it up I feel like a caterpillar that goes into its chrysalis and changes into a butterfly. The metamorphosis cannot happen without the chrysalis. Without it the caterpillar cannot turn into the beautiful butterfly. I need my chrysalis for now.

    5:09 I just checked my mail and I found a check from the State of Arizona for over payment for $458. I was down to my last ten dollars and my gas tank was on empty. It's amazing how things keep working out for me in perfect timing. Now I can give Frida back the $173.00 for the insurance. Maybe my Federal refund will come sooner than expected as well, and I can pay her back for the rent. At least now I can go buy food. I am getting a little tired of noodles. I also got a notice in the mail yesterday from Direct TV that they are giving me the Showtime channels for free for 12 months because I am a valued customer. Now I don't have to rent movie for a whole year.

> 7/10/09 Last night I dreamt that I met this beautiful blonde woman up at my dad's old cottage. We went on a boat ride on the lake in her dad's boat and we made love in the cabin of the boat. We took the boat to her cottage on the lake. Swam in the water, watched a cooking show, had some beer and we made love again. We were so in love in the dream that when I woke up I felt the love. I feel like I just met someone and fell in love. It feels that real.

    I had an interesting experience last night. I was very happy and I decided to watch two of my cowboy movies. These are movies that I would watch and get drunk and wish I could be the mean no named man that came into town and kicked everybody's ass and was afraid of nothing. However, last night I had some wine, I was in a happy mood, and I actually sat down and enjoyed the movies for the beautiful pieces of art that they are and I was able to delve into the meanings, metaphors, and lessons the movies were trying to teach. I really got involved and into them deeply. It was a wonderful experience and it was a first for me. I got a little drunk, but I had fun. I really enjoyed myself and the movies without feeling sad, depressed and lonely. Wow, another change in behavior for me.

I have also been thinking about love lately, especially after the dream I had last night. I really want to get to know a woman not just for her outer beauty, but her inner beauty. I want to know and be intimate with her inner self. I feel like I cannot have intercourse again until I find that relationship with a woman and know that it's her I really want to be with. I want to share that deep emotion and intimacy of our inner selves while making love. That's special between two people and that's what I want and that's what I want to experience. I feel like if I was to go out with someone and have sex with them before I get to know this inner person it's just that, sex. You feel good for a moment and then it passes. Then you fell guilty like I was being selfish and not only not having respect for myself, but not having respect for the other person. I want to find that deep beauty and intimacy and experience something that powerful and good that lasts and gets better as time goes on.

This makes me ponder about all the people I see in relationships today. They seem shallow and based on sex and physical attractiveness only. You can see and tell these relationships are false and won't last. Why can't they see it themselves? The world is much too materialistic for me these days. I think this really begs the question, how often do you see two people who are really in love? The last time I saw it was with my grandparents on my mom's side of the family. They were truly in love. You could see it in everything they did and there was no question about it.

Has our society really changed that much since that generation? Have we really become that hollow and shallow that true love for a human being is gone from our genre of emotions we have as humans? Are we becoming less human? Does it show us that our internal spirit is dead and does that then mean mankind is on its way to extinction? I wonder.

7/13/09 I had a dream that I was at my dad's house and we started a fire in the fire place. Then he wanted me to check the attic to see of it was on fire. So, I did and he started yelling at me. So, I got right back in his face and yelled at him. There were all of the people there that knew me since I was a child but I did not know them. I would go from room to room and they all were being remodeled. It was like I was trapped in there and couldn't get out. My mother was there to. There was part of the house that had a new bee hive fire place in it. It looked like one of those fancy rich houses, but it was very dark and it was raining outside through the whole dream.

7/14/09 Last night I dreamt I was living back at my dad's house and we were all up for work in the morning making our lunches. The rest of the kids started eating mine and I got pissed off at them and then my step mom and dad got mad at me. Then we went to work and I had to roll out these two long tapes down this dirt patch and keep these two ladies from taking them. When I got to the end other boss came out and measured some watermelons and said, "Good we have them all." We all got these fresh baked warm cookies to eat. I then went on to do the rest of job and we had to cross this sandy dusty area under a bridge and the wind picked up and it was blowing so much dust we had to stop and over our mouths with our scarves. Then, the boss came and got us and we got these makeshift marking guns we had to put together, but no one would show me how to do anything. It was at this point I got two new pairs of boots for work. We had to choose which ones we wanted. There was a construction boot type with treds and a type with smooth soles. I took the construction boot ones with all different treds on them. Then we had to put on a bigger boot than that over them, put our marking guns together, and the whole crowd of us had to go mask the metal locks. They were all pushing and shoving, there were people from my past, from Junior High, who were teasing me. But I gave it right back and I continued on with my job and got it done. I then woke up.

Well the weekend was exciting to say the least I am still recovering from it. Frida came over Friday night and I had miraculously received my tax check so I wanted to take her someplace nice to thank her for helping me out. We went to a fancy steak house and had a great meal, but we got a little tipsy. But, it was fun. I did not get sad or depressed. I was just having fun. The next day I felt a little like crap but I was ok.

Frida spent the night and she had assumed she was going to stay Saturday night as well and I felt a little threatened by that, but I got over it once I saw she was disappointed that I didn't want her to stay. I then got the idea to go to the grocery store and get some hotdogs and stuff to make margaritas and go down to the pool and have Chicago dogs on the grill. Frida liked that idea. So, that's what we did. We even met a few people down at the pool that we shared our hotdogs and margaritas with.

Only problem was that I was in the pool the whole day and didn't realize how drunk I was. I was having so much fun I didn't think to monitor how much I had. So, when I got out of the pool I fell straight down and bounced my head off of the concrete like a superball off of the wall. I was ok, but left with some bruises and a bit embarrassed. I was having so much fun. For once I was enjoying myself and others and not just using alcohol to numb my pain. Although on Sunday morning I certainly could have used something to numb the pain in my head and body, whew!

On Monday, I was still hurting so I spent the day recovering and sleeping I couldn't make it to therapy I was still feeling way to ill from my little trip to Margaretville.

Today I checked my email and I was feeling substantially better and there was an email from my boss telling me that my family medical leave act status will be up on July 17th, which is only three days away and I will have to come back to work. I got pissed and depressed and started thinking negative thoughts like, "Great I can't finish therapy, I can't finish this book."

However, after doing this for a good part of the afternoon I caught myself doing it and I remembered Eckhart Tolle's book, *The New Earth*. So, I pulled it out and read several pages I had marked which really caught my attention the first time I read it. I then got back to thinking I need to stay in the present. I have quoted the words I read, which struck me so deeply below:

> There is always this one step, and so you give it your fullest attention. This doesn't mean that you don't know where you are going; it just means this step is primary, the destination secondary. And what you encounter at your destination once you get there depends on the quality of this one step. Another way of putting it: what the future holds for you depends on your state of consciousness now."

Once I read this part my thinking began to change immediately and I remembered how just two weeks ago I was focused on this way of thinking and my writing and how when I was down to my last ten dollars, behind on the rent, and day care payments to my ex, because I was now on unpaid leave, my tax returns from the state and federal government came in and my doctor wouldn't release me to go back to work for another eight weeks. I thought I must get realigned and get into the now and then I read another paragraph in Tolle's book that really struck me:

> "Enjoyment of what you are doing combined with a goal or a vision that you work toward becomes enthusiasm. Even though you have a goal, what you are doing in the present moment needs to remain the focal point of your attention; otherwise, you will fall out of alignment with universal purpose. Make sure your vision or goal is not an inflated image of yourself and

therefore a concealed form of ego, such as wanting to become a movie star, a famous writer, or a wealthy entrepreneur. Also make sure your goal is not focused on having this or that, such as a mansion by the sea, your own company, or ten million dollars in the bank. An enlarged image of yourself or a vision of yourself having this or that are all static goals and therefore don't empower you. Instead, make sure our goals are dynamic, that is to say, point toward an activity that you are engaged in and through which you are connected to other human beings as well as to the whole. Instead of seeing yourself as a famous actor and writer and so on, see yourself inspiring countless people with your work and enriching their lives. Feel how that activity enriches or deepens not only your life but that of countless others. Feel yourself being an opening through which energy flows from the unmanifested source of all life through you for the benefit of all."

Once I got done reading that I became inspired and said to myself that I am going to stay focused on the now and what I want to do, which is write. So, I got back to work on my writing and not worrying about the future and then my phone rang. The caller ID said restricted and I wasn't going to answer it but my inner self told me I needed to. So, I answered the phone and it was the lady from our personnel department telling me that, "While yes my FMLA would be up July 17th, my doctor has not released me to go back to work for eight weeks. Therefore, even though the FMLA will be up I will not be returning to work until my doctor releases me to do so.

I hung up the phone in amazement. Just ten simple minutes after changing my focus and getting back to staying focused on the now and my goal of writing a book to help and inspire others the lady from personnel calls and gives me that news! Now, is that inspiring or what! I was so amazed and blown away that I had to call Frida and let her know what just had happened.

7/15/09 5:23am Well, I awoke again at 4:30am for two days in a row now. It's like my inner self is waking me up, saying, "get up, get up, it's time to write." Like I am some sort of vehicle for it to pass words through so that I may put them down on paper. It's weird the words just come to me and I write them down. The words, they come from the energy or being within me, if you will, and flow through me. The mornings are peaceful calm, and surreal. It is like the first day of creation. Everything is new, quiet. The birds are just now waking up sounding the alarm for breakfast. The old saying must be true; the early bird does get the worm.

The paper boy just passed by and it reminded me of when I still owned the houses in the city and out in the desert and I had to get a second job as a paper boy to try to make ends meet. I remember getting up at 2am and working till 5:30am and then going to get breakfast and catching a quick nap on the couch before going to my real job at 7:30am and working until 5pm, some nights even later.

The paper route was seven days a week. I had no time to enjoy anything. All I did was work. I was so caught up in money and trying to be rich. I was miserable. I was missing out on so much. I worked myself to the bone, so obsessed with money, until I got sick and had a nervous breakdown. Now, I can find peace, solace, and pure happiness in the peace and quiet when I write at 5:30 in the morning. The only things that are up now are the birds, the old man who swims in the pool every morning and me. Sometimes that old man reminds me of how some people live their lives and I've done it too. They just go in circles getting nowhere like the man swimming in the pool. He just goes round and round for 10 minutes and he is done.

It must be sad to live a life getting nowhere, not finding pure enjoyment and pleasure in the things you do. Why do we put ourselves through all the pain and agony of having these jobs we don't really want to do for the possession of material things? Why do we spend the majority of our lives doing things we don't like to only be able to spend some time doing what makes us happy? Why isn't it the other way around? That would seem to make more sense to me. But it's our obsession with material things. We think having things, lots of things will make us happy. We do not realize the true happiness comes from within when you are doing what you truly enjoy, what you are truly supposed to be doing, whose sole purpose in the end is not to be wealthy, but for the betterment of mankind. When you are doing that, you get all of the other things. It is being focused on "what" you are supposed to be doing and not on "what" you get from it that makes the difference. It is perfectly normal to want things, but you can't put the cart before the horse.

Well, it is now approaching 6am and my peaceful bliss is passing. The world has awoken and I must take my blood pressure and my medicine and spend some time typing up the pages of this book I am writing, or I will never get finished with it.

> 7/16/09 Last night I dreamt I was with my dad and two uncles and we were dressed like cowboys. We went to the old cottage. When we got there it looked like a house that was built in the old west. Half of the inside had fallen into serious disuse and was covered with spider webs and spiders everywhere. The other half of the house had been turned into a store that was selling old western things to tourists. The people who were running the store were happy and had smiles on their faces and I asked one of them if they got much business and he said, "No, but they were happy." I walked into one room and there were birds trapped in spider webs hanging from the ceiling. I kept running into all of these spiders and spider webs and I was freaking out. We then got in the car and drove down a road for a while that turned into a bad dirt road that had a lot of sharp 90 degree angle turns into it. We ended up at a bar, walked in and everyone else walked

down the stairs, but I jumped down. We went up to the bar and ordered a draft beer, but all they had were bottles. The lady wanted to see my ID and I got upset and I took off my hat and the guy behind the bar said I was ok and I said thanks and woke up.

6:13am The dream that I had last night had an impact on me. It was as if it was telling me that things have their time and place and some things fall into disuse and others find new purposes. I think it was telling me that my purpose is now changing and that I am ok, I am doing well. I ran into a lot of spiders and spider webs in my dream of which I have been told means wealth, success and richness. I think it means a wealth in everything in life.

I sit here every morning now at 5:30am on the balcony of my apartment and meditate in the early morning stillness. I practice being still in body and mind as the world begins to wake up. I find great peace in these moments. It is almost as if it feels like the beginning of time and all things are just being created, just coming to life.

I usually have great clarity of mind at this time and writing comes very freely to me before the mind gets cluttered with the day's events. It is like I get this great urge to write that I just can't resist and the words just come to me as if God himself is whispering them into my ear. I sit here and wonder how many people actually get up this early and enjoy these precious moments of peace and try to connect with their spirit? Not many I suspect these days, as everyone is in pursuit of their material things. I feel sorry for those who miss the peace I find at this time in the morning and the great joy it brings me to meditate and connect with my inner spirit, or energy, if you will. You can't put a monetary value on that. I feel far richer than they who live in a mansion on top of the mountain.

Even though physically I appear to be alone, I never feel that way. My spirit, which is comprised of the same energy as God is always here with me. I know this especially because I take the time to feel it. I listen to it when it speaks to me, and I have learned to trust it even when it speaks to me in my dreams.

The world is an amazing place and we, as humans, are incredibly amazing creatures with such special abilities. Yet, most people are just so dead. It is like they are shells and they operate like robots negating not only the beauty and amazement the world has to offer, but negating their own miraculous beauty within. I feel a deep sadness for these people, such that it pains me to write this truth. Why don't they wake up? Why don't they see? What are they scared of? If only they could believe.

> 7/19/09 Last night I dreamt that I was a student at ASU and we were having a championship football game. We were all at the game dressed in our colors and I was standing on the sidelines with some black guys and the coach from the other team told us to back off and called the black people a nasty name and we had to jump down in the entry way to the tunnel where we couldn't see the game. Our coach came over and argued with their coach but ended up backing down and we missed seeing the game, but we won and I got a bunch of free ASU jerseys and one of the opposite team, but it had footprints all over it and I then woke up.

9:50am Well, this weekend has been an emotionally distraught one for me. Last Thursday my buddy from Prescott came down on business and he wanted to go out to dinner. Frida was going to come over and make tacos, but we met my friend for dinner instead and we talked about some issues he is having in his life right now.

We then parted ways and while Frida and I were sitting here at home I just became overwhelmed with emotion. I had to tell her I have all of these emotions for Muslim women and that I had talked to Sakeen. I was just overwhelmed. I had to say something or I was going to explode. I just needed to let the feelings out to someone. She was a little upset and questioned our relationship. All I could tell her was I don't know what it is right now. I am just getting flooded with the emotions of compassion and love and that I don't understand it, and I don't know why all of a sudden. Maybe it's because I am becoming human again, my feelings are coming back and these were particular emotions that I have really suppressed my whole life because I never got them from anyone.

I then told her all I know is right now I just need a friend and that's all I can say. I am just very confused and I am trying to figure out how to handle this big influx of raw emotion. I am still finding out who I am I guess. I probably really never knew who I was because of everything I have been through, everything I have suppressed; I never really got the chance to get to know me.

She then seemed to be ok with it. She went to bed and I stayed up all night drinking because now I felt bad for dumping all of that on her and I just felt horrible like I always do when I get these suppressed emotions out. I always get sad and drink after that before I feel better.

Frida went to work on Friday. I slept most of the day and I still belt horrible so I drank again and stayed up until 3am while all of this emotion was coming out. It's all just happening so fast, it's like I can't, or better yet, don't know how to handle it.

I then slept all day Saturday. I got up Saturday evening and went for a beer. I grabbed one, ate some food and decided I would watch something on TV to get my mind off of things. I decided that this weekend was going to be different. I would not spend the whole weekend drinking because I don't know how to handle my feelings and I think I do it because it is a learned behavior that I taught myself to do to numb myself from my emotions and memories as a young man. I need to find a better way. I need to re-focus on what I am supposed to be doing; writing my book. So, I quit drinking beer, had some tomato juice and watched this great show on Borneo on one of the science channels. I then read for ½ an hour, meditated and fell asleep by 10:30pm. I slept all the way through until 8:30am today. My medicine really knocked me out last night.

I got up, had a cup of coffee outside and began to work on my book as I had planned. So, I guess this is a victory for me. I changed my behavior over the weekend. I beat it. I did not stay drunk trying numb myself because that's all I knew how to do and because it was the easiest way. I re-focused and turned to something else. I am proud of myself. I did well on Saturday. Yes, this deserves a pat on the back to myself. I think I will have steak for dinner tonight to treat myself!

> 7/20/09 5:39pm Well, I guess I can take my pat on the back away. I didn't have a steak last night. Frida had come over and made tacos and we began to talk. I was still feeling depressed from this onslaught of feelings I was still going through, like love, attraction, loneliness. She then told me we were just friends and it went downhill from there. We ended up not eating and she left. I sat outside all night drinking. There was a storm rolling in so it was cloudy and it was lightening so the horizon was lighting up like it did during the war and the thunder sounded like the bombs being dropped and there was a guy down at the pool speaking Arabic, so all of those things just added to my problems and made things a hell of a lot worse for me.

I saw the sun come up again, which is like the second or third time for me in the last few days. I finally made it to bed at around 8am after taking my morning medications and I slept until 2pm, and went back to bed and just woke up a few minutes ago. I am still so tired and drained and I am lonely just being here in this apartment all by myself all of the time. I have no money to go anywhere. All I do is work on my book. Some company would be nice, but I doubt that's going to happen. So, I didn't go to therapy today for obvious reasons but I see my psychiatrist tomorrow afternoon.

> 7/21/09 9:38am I am completely drained still from this emotional bombardment that I have been going through the last several days. I slept from 10pm until 9am this morning and I probably could have slept

longer, but I made myself get up. I am being overloaded with these feelings of compassion and love and I am seeing beauty in people I have never seen before. Sometimes, I feel like a high school kid falling in love all over again.

I talk to Frida about these things because we are still friends, but then I feel bad because when she was my girlfriend I didn't have all of these feelings towards her, but we could never talk then either and she's learning to now. So, after I go through this onslaught of feelings of love, compassion, and seeing beauty in people, I look around the apartment and see that I am alone and I get depressed as hell and I feel guilty about telling Frida about this stuff, but I have to let it out because I feel like I will explode if I don't. Then I end up staying up all night and not taking my m medicine and then sleep all day and then I am just so tired and soar that I just lay in bed depressed and wondering what the hell is going on with me, when will I feel good again like a normal person. Then sometimes I can't take feeling like this and I drink. I feel like I am caught in this big cycle and can't get out, like a rat stuck in a wheel.

12:16pm I have got it! I am on a journey to recovery and it is up and down and this journey is what my book is about! I want people to realize you can get better and that a lot of these self-help books are good for you, but none of them show you what recovery is actually like! They tell you how to do it, but they don't actually show you what it's like so you know if you're going down the right path or not, in order to help you keep going when you do hit the low points of recovery, which one will because the road to recovery is full of ups and downs like the stock market.

2:50pm I just got back from seeing my psychiatrist and we talked about these intense emotions I have towards Muslim women, or even one that looks similar. She said it was from my experiences in the war about the lady unveiled in the desert, the way they were oppressed, etc., she said it's the same thing as the camaraderie I had with my fellow Marines. She said it's a strong connection because we were both fighting the Iraqi's for freedom. She suggested not to act on these sudden strong impulses (like I did the other night by running downstairs and saying hi to this Muslim girl who was doing her laundry) but to go for a walk or something and then if by chance I run into a Muslim woman say, "Hello" maybe she will say hi back. She said it might be good for me to have a relationship with a Muslim woman, but it should be natural and not forced by my impulses. I really need to get out more and take her advice.

> 7/22/09 10:26am So, last night I was still going through my onslaught of emotions. So, I took the doctor's advice and went for a nice long swim. Then, I took a shower and walked down to the mall and bought myself a wonderful apple wood smoked Salmon dinner and I had some wine. I was there a couple hours and then I went to the bookstore and bought a few books and I got a cup of coffee. I sat in the café and started reading my book. So, for a few hours my mind was taken off of my flashbacks and I left the bookstore café at 11pm and walked home. I took my medicine and laid down. But, to no avail I could not get any sleep. I just laid there thinking about the emotional assault I was still going through. I just kept going through these feelings of love and compassion for these Muslim women like I have the strong connection with them and then after that it turns into depression as I am left all alone in reality.

While I was lying in bed from 1am until 2am I was having this battle with myself about whether or not I should just go get some beer and numb this shit and fall asleep. But, I kept telling myself, "No, I have to let myself experience this or it will only come back worse next time!"

I got up and went downstairs to the Jacuzzi and sat in that for a while thinking that would tire me out, especially after my medicine. But, it did not. I went back upstairs to my apartment and laid back down still fighting the argument to go get beer and get some sleep. Finally at 2am I lost the battle. I got up, got dressed, and walked down to the store, but when I got there at 2:10am I found out they quit serving alcohol at 2am. So, I had to walk all the way back home. I sat on my balcony in the monsoon breeze and ate sunflower seeds for a while and then I decided to lay back down.

 I finally fell asleep at sunup and slept until 9am, about four hours. I had missed my group therapy and started beating myself up for that. But I had to accept that this is the way I feel right now, this is what I am going through at the moment. Its ok, therapy is tough. I have to remember that I am working on getting better and I am making progress. I have to quit being impatient and remember it takes time. I have to let this stuff come out so I can bet better. It's just weird to go from having flashbacks about combat and horrid things to having flashbacks of feeling love, compassion, and a deep attachment to Muslim women. But, the doctor said it was normal. It is just hard for me to comprehend especially when I get hit with all of these emotions at once.

 11:07am I just saw the same Muslim girl walk by that I said hi to the other night and I got this incredible impulse to run down there and say hi to her, but like the doctor said, "Don't act on those sudden impulses, that's what you do when you have flashbacks." So, I just sat on my balcony and watched her go by and hoped that someday by chance we might meet each other and strike up a nice conversation.

 2:21pm I went running to burn off some negative energy and then when I cooled off, I meditated for about a half an hour. I feel more peaceful now. I am going to eat and get back to reading my book.

 4:55pm After reading my book for a while I began to ponder the journey of my life. I think about my childhood getting beat up and picked on at school, then going home to getting yelled at, screamed at, and hit. I think about how that prepared me for the Marine Corps and how they took it one step further and prepared me for, and sent me to, war. And, how that turned into writing a book about my experiences, meeting a woman who had my baby only to leave me and take all my money in child support and how that led me to the pursuit of being rich and working my ass off and owning two houses, meeting Frida, then going through financial disaster, bankruptcy, ending up in the hospital with six weeks off of work to only end up in another hospital a year later because of a suicidal ideation due to my PTSD returning and Frida's willingness to take me there.

It is through those experiences that I met counselors and doctors who have guided me toward the true meaning of life and the pursuit of one's true passion and when you do that how the universe conspires to work with you and provide for you. I don't know what is coming next, I know something is, but I must focus on the present and my messages will be revealed to me and it is what I do in this present moment that helps determine what happens in the future. I live and wait and see! And this learning of life has created an obsession in me to learn more of the truth and to write about my journey. It is my passion; it is what I must now do and I am excited to see where this part of my life leads me next!

> 7/23/09 12:46pm I just finished reading my book and I take its message to be: "Follow your intuition (your heart) once you find your heart there will be your treasure." I need to find my heart. This is what my journey is about. Maybe that's what those three war dreams I always had where I got wounded in the chest and died were about. They were saying I needed to find and follow my heart and once I did, I would quit dying.

I have this intuition to sit on my balcony all afternoon in the heat and fast to purify myself until dark time. I must become pure of heart and soul. I must teach myself to be still and find peace. I can't explain it. It is just something I am being told by my inner self to do and that once I do that the answers will come.

1:41pm I just talked to the counselor at the hospital and since I missed a week I almost got dropped from group therapy; however, I think I will be ok at least that's what the counselor seems to think since we talked on the phone. More importantly she said she is doing research on trauma and PTSD and she's working on putting a group together and wanted to know if I would like to be on a call back list to be a part of it. I said I would. I have been talking about trying to find a way to give back to the hospital and also help people and Veterans and then this pops up out of the blue. Weird, it is amazing how things are just happening in their own due time. Like Tolle and Coelho say, "When you follow your passion the universe conspires to help you!"

5:44pm Well, I fasted all day and sat on my balcony and sweated out all the bad in me. I just have to make it until tomorrow now without eating and then my demonstration of intention of getting rid of my bad crap will be done.

7/24/09 Last night I dreamt that I had to testify in court and the judge and the entire jury were all women and I was nervous standing up in front of the judge and I couldn't stop my leg from shaking. I then woke up.

7/28/09 7:24am Well I had a great time with my son this weekend. We watched dinosaur movies, wrestled, went to dinner and read books. He is so smart at five years old. It really is amazing. He is such a bundle of energy. Thank God for ibuprofen! It's Tuesday and I am still soar! Yesterday I went to therapy and the rest of the day I was just kind of depressed still about the Muslim woman thing. For some reason I am very attracted to the girl I said hello to the other night and I don't know why I am attracted to her in particular. But I decided that I was just going to accept the fact that I was depressed yesterday and feel it and let it out and not try to bury it like I usually do. I feel somewhat better today.

3:19pm I just got back from the doctor and I am completely depressed. We talked about being in the war and all the awful things we did and how the people didn't want us there and how our own government used us as guinea pigs for drugs and to crawl through minefields. She made me talk about how it makes me feel. Well, it sucks! That is how it feels and it leaves you feeling horribly guilty, sad, and depressed. We also talked about my attraction to Muslim women and we got down to the point that I am looking for forgiveness from them and I want to say I am sorry for what I did. So, now I feel like crap again. So, she upped my medicine to 60mg from 40mg. Oh well, at least I felt ok this morning. This is part of the roller coaster ride of recovery. Actually it is more like a graph of the stock market, constantly up and down.

I talked to the City on Friday and it appears that my disability has been approved, so I am quite happy about that. Now, I can continue writing. My lease will be up in a couple weeks so I have to decide if I am going to stay in the apartment I am in or move into a studio, which would be a couple hundred bucks cheaper. I really don't feel like moving, but it may be a choice I should make in order to save some money. It's a pain in the butt for me to have to change addresses and all that stuff, especially with the child support and the fact that I just filed for disability through Social Security as a requirement of the City.

8:19pm Well, the trash can if full of beer bottles again. Goodnight people!

7/29/09 3:48pm This morning the Muslim lady that lives on the third floor across from me came out and started praying on her mat on her balcony. I was sitting on my balcony trying to drink some coffee. I watched her. It was a beautiful thing to watch. She finished and went inside and got a chair and her laptop and she sat outside. I kept watching her. Just then her husband (I think) came outside and said, "What are you doing?" and she quickly scurried back in the house. I felt awful. I felt like the incident with the

Muslim lady in the war happened all over again just because he saw me he made his wife go inside, at least that's how I felt. I was angry at him and wanted to punch him because of what he had done to his wife, yet at the same time, I felt guilty and depressed like I do when I think about what we did in the war.

I am talking about all of this stuff in therapy and these things keep happening that remind me of incidents from the war and I am flooded with all these emotions of guilt, anger, depression, loneliness, hopelessness, and fear. I know it is good to let it out, but I have to find a way to rise above it now. Just letting it out is not good enough anymore. Sitting here depressed and drinking beer all afternoon after every time I let something out has to stop. I have to face this, experience it, but in healthy ways. I have been reading this poem by Paulo Coelho over and over today. It is inspirational to me and sums up what I need to do pretty well I think. It is as follows:

> The warrior of the light unwittingly takes a false step and plunges into the abyss. Ghosts frighten him and solitude torments him. His aim had been to fight the good fight, and he never imagined that this would happen to him, but it did. Shrouded in darkness, he makes contact with his master.
>
> "Master, I have fallen into the abyss," he says. "The waters are deep and dark." "Remember one thing," replies his master. "You do not drown by simply plunging into the water; you only drown if you stay beneath the surface." And the warrior uses all his strength to escape from his predicament.

This is what I need to do, rise above the waters I have plunged into! Perhaps I need to come up with a new schedule, such as running on the days I don't have group. I can take my night meds earlier in the evening so I can get to sleep sooner, relax sooner, and then I can get up earlier and write! That is when I like to write, very early in the morning. I can do this on non-group days and then run in the late morning. Then on all days I can spend my afternoons reading and quenching my thirst for knowledge. I can slip in all of my chores and any social things in between there. I also want to make sure that I meditate three times a day, first thing in the morning, in the middle of the day and then in the evening before bed. Yes, I think this new, revised schedule will work. I am much deeper into my recovery now and further along with my therapy. I am revealing and dealing with some very deep emotional trauma from the war now that I haven't allowed to surface in 20 years. So, think I must do like the athlete does when he or she gets into a slump, analyze what is happening, make the necessary adjustments, and try again!

> 7/30/09 6:25am Well, so far my new plan is working I awoke at 4:30 this morning, made coffee, meditated, sat and watched the sun come up, took my blood pressure and my morning medicine. I am still waiting to see if the Muslim lady across from me is going to come out and pray. She should have been outside by now as the sun is getting higher over the horizon. Maybe she really did get in trouble from her husband yesterday for being outside. Could he really be that upset at her because I saw her? That doesn't make me feel real good. I feel sorry for her to have to be treated that way, but I suppose it's none of my business.

The birds are all coming to life now. Earlier I saw a whole flock of geese flying east across the sky towards the lakes over at the golf course just after sun up. It was beautiful. Its amazing birds that big can fly so gracefully. Today I have another round of therapy and then I will get a three day break from it, which will be nice.

8/02/09 Last night I dreamt that my sister, dad and I were on vacation on this boat that was docked next to this naval base. I went swimming in the water and a Navy ship was leaving the harbor. So I was trying to swim back in but the waves and current were very strong. My dad yelled from the boat that I would really have to kick to make it back to the boat. So, I really swam hard and put everything I had into it and made it back to the boat. Then we had to leave because the Navy was kicking us out because they were changing the batteries of all the submarines in the submarine division.

I also dreamt I was at my uncle's house and we were supposed to go camping, but we had a talk instead. He asked me if it was ok if we took it easy for a while because he was getting into too much trouble drinking and driving, smoking, and cheating on his wife. I cried in the dream.

1:09 Well, its Sunday and I had another setback. I am ok with it though. I realize it's going to happen from time to time. I drank beer and watched my war movies, got depressed and didn't take my night meds. I had a rough week last week and still keep hearing Steven's voice from therapy "give yourself a break, you've been through hell!" I have and this is going to happen from time to time. It is expected to have this happen when you're on the road to recovery.

So, this week I am going to set some small goals and only think about the week and getting through it. First of all, I am not going to have any beer from Sunday until next Sunday and then I will reanalyze that situation at that time. I didn't get my disability check from the City last week like they said I would so I hope I get it Monday so I can pay my damn rent.

Anyhow, the second thing this week that I want to do is make sure I meditate three times a day. Thirdly, on Monday, Wednesday, and Thursday I want to swim after group therapy to help get rid of the negative energy. Then on Tuesday, Friday, and Saturday in the late morning, before it gets too hot, I want to run. Then, with the rest of my time I will write, read, and watch some TV. I will make it to all three group therapy sessions this week and to my appointment with my psychiatrist on Monday. I will also make sure that I take all of my meds properly and to take the night ones by 7pm so I can be to bed early so I can get up early. So, we will see how this goes. Next Sunday I will re-evaluate how I feel and how everything went.

> 8/03/09 6:54am I woke up all pissed off this morning at myself. I slept like shit on top of it and I am mad because I allowed myself to get off of my routines last week and especially over the weekend. When is all of the emotional crap going to stop? I have had enough already. I had a hard time meditating and falling asleep last night and then I tried to meditate this morning but it just wasn't happening there were too many thought racing through my head and I was too pissed off. I just took my meds so we will see if they do anything for me.

3:44pm, I am done with my therapy marathon for the day. I had a good session with my psychiatrist. She had to remind me that I spent 20 years being numb, that there is 20 years of damage; it will take time to repair it. I can't expect to have gone to therapy for three months and be better. It doesn't work that way. She said it may take a year, two, or several years, she doesn't know. So I guess I need to let myself succumb to the fact that it's going to take time and I need to understand that I am doing exactly what I should be doing at exactly the time I should be doing it.

The doctor said that I have made progress and she can tell because all of these emotions are coming up and I am feeling them versus being numb like I had been for 20 years. I guess she is right. She increased another one of my meds from one milligram to two milligrams because I have been having trouble sleeping all week. I do feel better though after talking to her and getting a little pep talk. She really is a good doctor. I am glad I found her.

She also told me at least I am doing something about my problems and unfortunately, this is how you have to deal with it. You have to talk about it, face it, and relive it in order to desensitize the emotional aspect of it so it just becomes a memory instead of an emotionally charged memory.

> 8/04/09, 7:18am Last night, with the increase in my medication, I slept a lot better. I only woke up once at 3:30am and I actually slept from 8:45pm until 6am. That felt good after not sleeping well for the last two weeks.

10:02am The day is going pretty well. I am in a decent mood and I feel like I will be able to maintain it through the rest of the day. Plus, I had a good night's sleep. I have been working on my book, getting my chores done, and maybe the increase in medicine is starting to help. I was bad last night and had two beers before dinner. So, tonight at about 5pm or 5:30pm I am going to go on my run, come back, take a shower, make dinner, eat, take my meds and relax for the night with a good book or TV. The theory being I am replacing the beer with something more productive and healthier for me.

> 8/05/09 Last night I dreamt that I was in some kind of hospital or treatment program and it was this girl and my turn to count the money. There were several different kinds of money to count up and there was a lot of it. We kept getting interrupted by people and confused and we couldn't count the money. At one point we even lost some of the money. Some of the guys there were poking fun at me and eventually at 9pm at night we got the money counted. Then one of the counselors came in and said, "Tomorrow at 10am is your last meal here folks." I then woke up.

11:38am Last night Frida and I went out for pizza and I ended up having a few glasses of wine. However, we had a good time and we had the same waitress we had before whom keeps flirting with me. She is a very attractive Native American woman. I am not sure if she really likes me or if she is just fishing for tips. So, I am going to have to go back in there by myself one night and ask her out and see what happens. I talked to Frida about all of this. She was real good about it. It was her idea for me to go back there by myself sometime. I felt bad for talking to her about stuff like that, but I explained to her that I need a friend like that right now and that I do love her very much. It's just that with all the changes that are happening to me I feel like a new person who is experiencing the world for the first time so I want to try everything. It's like I got a second chance and I want to take advantage of it.

8/11/09, 6:44am I haven't written in a few days. I went up to Prescott to visit my buddy from high school and his family. We had a boy's night out on Friday which was fun and we went to his wife's parents on Saturday for a barbecue, which was also fun.

My depression had gone away after seeing my doctor on last Monday; however, on Friday I became irritable and angry and I got anxious and I have been like that ever since, just going off on minor things. I had therapy yesterday and I also saw my doctor and she gave me some things to try when I get these overwhelming emotions and how to let them go. I tried it last night, but I really didn't feel much of a change. But, I will keep trying. She said I would need to practice it. She also told me to think about what I want to do in the future with myself when I am better and we would talk about it next week.

8/13/09 11:49am Tuesday night I went to the pizza place by my house. I wanted to ask out one of the waitresses there that has been flirting with me; however, she wasn't there, but I made a new friend, which seemed a bit fortuitous to me in that we got to talking and she told me she just travels. She follows her dreams and she told me not to be afraid to follow mine. So, I made a new friend and had a good time.

Then, I stayed up late watching movies and drinking beer. I got up the next day which was around 11am and had coffee. At about 1pm my neighbors whom I met a while back were out partying at the pool so they called me down to party with them in the pool. So, I did, all day. I came home and watched another movie, went to bed at 3am and now it's almost noon and I just got up. I am really turning into a social butterfly now. I am talking to everyone, hanging out with new people, making new friends. It's great. I am even flirting with girls now. I feel so open and new. It's like I just got this new toy and I can't stop playing with it. I missed group yesterday and today and I don't think I am going to go back. I think I have gotten about all I can get out of it. It's not like I need to tell them every single one of my stories. I have told them a lot already and made many breakthroughs. There's not much more I can do there. I will do the finishing work with my psychiatrist and my therapist. It's time for me to be spending most of my time on my own in the world and not in therapy all day long.

I have been partying a lot with people as well, which, is something I always felt had been taken away from me by my time spent in the Marine Corps and the war. I spent my 21st birthday in combat. So, even though I probably shouldn't be doing it for health reasons, I feel it's something I must do for me and my mental health and need to go do these things and get them out of my system. I have to say, if feels pretty good.

8/17/09 8:02am I had a great weekend. I have been feeling better lately practicing the techniques that my psychiatrist taught me about how to experience and let go of emotions and to think about what I want to do with my life. I went camping on the Mogollon Rim with Frida. It was great to be outdoors. We saw a vulture, two blue jays, a Horny toad, humming birds, and two white tail deer. The weekend break was nice and refreshing. I left a message for the therapist who ran my group therapy on Friday that I won't be back to group. I am going to spend the day writing today, but I have some paperwork I need to fill out and mail off, plus I also want to try and get in a run today.

10am What do we mean when we talk about a man's soul? Is the collective body of energy that flows through our bodies transmitted by our brain? But, then where does the brain get these ideas or the impetus to transmit electrical signals throughout the body? And, why is it that most people ignore these ideas? This writing that I am doing now is just flowing through me. It's coming from my soul and my brain, but where are they getting it from?

I was asked in an Anthropology course once, "What is it that makes us human?" I thought, at the time, that it was our cognitive thinking skills. However, now I must refine my answer to say that what makes us human is the brain's ability to transmit messages to us, it can tell us what to do or say, it can even tell us what to write in a book. And, concomitant to that, we as human beings have the separate ability to accept or deny these messages sent by the brain.

However, if we accept them and act on them, are we then human and if we deny them does that make us incomplete human beings? I guess the answer would depend on where we believe the brain gets its messages from. Is it God? Who knows? I personally believe there is a supreme creator I like to call God. I think we all have a specific personal purpose for living this physical life and we also have a general purpose for hiving this physical life. In other words, we have something to accomplish and something to learn before we may enter an eternal bliss. And, we are given messages and signs all day and night to help guide us; however, most people ignore them.

I remember one night, back in the mid to late 1990's when my grandfather was sick and dying, I was lying in bed saying my prayers for the night. I had asked God to take care of my grandpa and to protect him.

The next day I learned that he had slipped and fallen in the driveway on his way to the mail box and hurt himself. I became very angry at God for not protecting him.

So, that next night when I went to bed I chewed God out for letting my grandpa fall and hurt himself. I looked at the clock one last time and it said it was 11:34pm and I fell asleep. Just as I fell asleep I was violently flipped over on to my back and I started to float up towards a light coming through the ceiling. My room was dark accept for this light. It was very windy inside my room and I was grasping at my blankets as I was floating, but I kept floating towards the light. I was scared half to death and I was desperately trying to do the sign of the cross on my chest, but I could not move a muscle.

Just before I floated into the light I managed to get my hand on my chest and complete the sign of the cross. As soon as I did that the light went away. I fell back on to my bed. My covers were all pulled into a pile in the middle of the bed. My eyes were watering and I was unable to move. Just then the feeling in my body came back and I was able to move. I turned to look at the clock thinking I had a nightmare, but the clock still said 11:34pm, which I realized upside down, on a digital clock, spells "hell". I was mortified.

One other time in 1997 I had passed out in a Denny's. My heart had stopped and I found out later that it had been stopped for a whole minute. However, what is truly unique about this is that once that happened I was floating in this black void up towards a light. I knew I was dead and I felt the most intense calm peace I have ever experienced and I said to myself, "I don't know why I was so scared of dying. It's really not that bad."

So, I know from personal experiences there is something else out there besides ourselves. And still even after those two experiences, it has taken me nearly twelve years to begin to trust and listen to it when it speaks to me.

8/18/09 10am I changed my routine up a bit. I want to make sure I get my runs in so I got up this morning, meditated, had a cup of coffee and then went running. I think I like this routine. Today I have to go visit my psychiatrist so we will see what I am like when I leave there. I have been in a pretty good mood this week focusing on my book and practicing the techniques the doctor taught me in order to release my emotions. I hope this good feeling hangs around for a while.

8/19/09 Last night I dreamt I was with my mom, step dad and half-sister and we went to Saudi Arabia. I bought a bunch of beans and chilies for our food and we entered a camel race and a marathon. So, I was taking some vitamins and my step dad said something to me and I repeated back to him what he had said, but then he did not believe me and I was getting mad. So my step dad asked my half-sister what he said and she agreed with him. I got madder and I then said, "I wouldn't trust her at all and that's not what you said." Then we were going to be late for the camel race and it was cold out so I got everyone clothes to wear from a vendor. I was very anxious about being late and trying to hurry and I woke up.

8/22/09 11:44am I have not written in a few days as I have been working on my book, running, and completing homework from my doctor. I have been doing very well this week and I have been working on interpreting my dreams I had recorded for the last six years based on Carl Jung's philosophy that dreams are full of symbols that mean something to us individually and thus represent repressed feelings disguised in order to trick our mind so that the feelings can come out or we would just repress them again. However, several of my dreams warn me or enlighten me to future events. It is becoming quite insightful and a very useful tool in my mental health to pay attention to my dreams.

I just recently interpreted a dream about a girl who was a very good friend of mine during my childhood and I had just now, at 39 years of age, realized the emotions that I had repressed back then and then I was able to let them out finally, experience them, and let them go; therefore, improving my mental health and lessening the mental baggage that I carry around with me. Dreams are indeed a useful tool in the arsenal of tools the mind has at its disposal. We can indeed use them in order to heal ourselves mentally. This sort of insight is not possible for any other creature on this planet that I know of and I really think this is something that makes us uniquely human.

8/24/09 Last night I had a continuation of a dream I had before. Before we were at this park and we were going to drive these race cares, but we had to get things like a helmet and stuff and a driving suit and put it in a locker that was going to be difficult to find. In this dream I was getting ready to race, it was our turn and I remembered I forgot to go to my locker and get my stuff, but I couldn't find it and I was in my underwear. Then someone stole all of my stuff and I started chasing him through this building where the lockers were, but I couldn't catch him and I ended up falling through four tarps layered like tin roofs and I woke up.

8/26/09 5:46am This morning I awoke at 4:30am. I got up and made coffee and sat outside on my balcony. As soon as the sun came up just like clockwork, the fat man who always swims in the morning arrived at the pool. He swims for 10 minutes and leaves. I watch people leave for work. Some of them are coming home from work. Yet, they all seem dead, like zombies or robots just walking around doing what they were programmed to do. There's no thinking involved. They are just moving along like ants. Is that what humans have become, a society of ants? We just go about our business, build our things and it's all done without emotion, compassion, or love. How did we get so numb, so narrow minded? We've been told since we were children, generation after generation, you go to school, get a job, work hard, buy a home, get married, raise a family and then die. So, like robots, we do it. But, there's never any mention of happiness in all of that. I guess it's because we assimilated happiness into material culture. If we acquire all of these things we will be happy right? Yet every now and then someone comes along who defies this, who has pure happiness and joy in their hearts and they just do what they love.

They spread peace like ST. Francis of Assisi; they create beautiful art like Leonardo Da Vinci, Van Gogh, or Renoir. They make great inventions like Thomas Jefferson and Thomas Edison, they achieve great things like Gorge Washington, Benjamin Franklin, or Teddy Roosevelt. They become great spiritual leaders like Mother Theresa, Mahatma Gandhi, or Petangelli. They create great books like Henry David Thoreau and Edgar Allen Poe, Dante and Charles Dickens.

There are great books written about these people; great works of art created. We hold them at a higher level than ourselves. It's like they have special abilities or, they are rare cases of human beings creating great and special things. But, they are not! They are merely a few cases of human beings actually being human beings and following their hearts desire, listening to their intuition and great things happen that bring peace, joy and happiness to the world.

We act like they are something special, but they're not. They are human beings just like you and I. Only, they follow their hearts instead of materialistic acquirements, which do eventually lead to sadness, stress, and despair because these things change and disappear with time. They come and go and since our identity is associated with them we suffer. We then become stricken with neurosis.

Yet, with all of these people I mentioned throughout history who have made great accomplishments, one thing has never changed. They followed their hearts and they spread peace, love and happiness to other human beings to enjoy for centuries to come, well after they have passed on. And this is something we are all able to do if we just pay attention to our hearts and our intuition.

> 9/02/09 3:54am Over the weekend I got a text message from my ex saying how often she thinks about us and how awful her life would be and how screwed up our son would be if she wasn't brave enough to leave me. I was devastated. The amount of cruelty that woman can inflict with her mouth never ceases to amaze me. So, I talked to the doctor about it yesterday and she made me realize I am never going to change her. She is just an awful person, just like I am never going to change my mother.

I have been trying to get recognition from my mother for 39 years, but I still don't get it. The doctor made me realize that I have spent 39 years, saying, "Hey I am here!" But, I got nothing back. I went in the Marine Corps, fought a war, put myself through college, got a steady job for 13 years, bought two houses, wrote a book, ran a marathon all just to get my mother's, or anyone's attention, but I got nothing.

Well, now it is time to let go of all of this crap and start doing things for myself. I have to realize that the only thing that really separates my son and I is distance on a map and that we are always together in our hearts and that when he gets older he will realize what has happened and what went on. I just need to keep being a good daddy to him and I know I am because he always says he wants to live with me and that we will be best friends forever. God, I love that little guy with all of my heart.

The older I get the more I learn how cruel human beings really are and as time goes on how it has become easier and easier for them to be nastier and more selfish. Look at the world we live in today. It is full of hate, greed, lust, war, pestilence, and starvation, but no one seems to give a damn unless they can use it as a campaign slogan to get elected to some sort of office. I had a good cry about all of this in the doctor's office yesterday and I really need to let go of all of these things and realize I can't change these people, they never will, but I want peace and I want to start doing things for me!

10:21am I started doing my homework for the doctor, which was releasing things that I want to change about my life. I have to feel the emotions and release them. I got to number eight on my list and started vomiting my guts out. These emotions were so intense for me that they actually made me sick as I was feeling and releasing them. So, needless to say I need a damn beer and I am taking a break for the day. Maybe I will just go ahead and get drunk and forget all about this crap for today.

> 9/07/09 10:14am I finally finished the homework the doctor gave me. It was a bit rough feeling those emotions and letting go of wanting to change all of the things that happened to me. They are done, so I leave them in the past. Now I have this list of goals I want to accomplish and I am trying to decide if I should just start with one and work my way through the list as I complete them or can I start and do a few things at the same time?

For instance I am writing this book and training for a full marathon at the same time. However, I am finding that both activities are full time commitments, so I think I need to decide which one to do first. The running often leaves me worn out and tired without the energy to do other things. So, I guess I will write this book first because if it gets published that will allow me to do, or at least help me, to do all of the other things I want to do.

I think I will do the full marathon second so I can devote all of my time to training properly. I can still exercise by running a few miles every day until I am done with the book, or maybe I won't.

When I keep thinking about doing more than one thing at once I begin to feel very overwhelmed. Why can't I get myself to just concentrate on one thing at a time? Well, I have decided to do just exactly that. One thing at a time for myself. Just like the exercise the doctor gave me to do, I don't have to impress anyone or even prove myself worth to myself. I have let go of trying to change all of that, so I am going to accomplish my goals one goal at a time just for myself because it's what I want to do now! So, here is my list of goals that I plan to accomplish:

- Write this book
- Be better off financially
- See a baseball game in every Major league ball park
- Go backpacking and explore my state
- Write music and play my guitar
- Run a full marathon
- Read all of the books I have
- Allow myself to have fun
- Own a nice boat in San Diego Harbor

I am looking at them as my new journey through life. It is with courageousness, acceptance, and peace that I emerged from my chrysalis to once again face the world and this time to live my life in peace and harmony!

After writing this book I have obviously spent a lot of time thinking about life and what it is. So, I have comprised a little poem that I think surmises my thoughts on the subject well and that I would like to leave you with:

-LIFE-
Living every moment in the now
Internal feelings that must be experienced some how
Forgiving yourself for your past
Experiencing things as they happen because they never last!

As life would have it, plans change a thousand times. The Marines always say, "Semper Gumby!" Always flexible. Shortly after I made this plan to live my life by, I moved in with Frida and her father in their house. Things were going good for me. I was sticking to my plan.

I wrote the first draft of this book, I went backpacking with Frida in the mountains around our state and we practiced living off of the land while we did it. I wrote music, took guitar lessons and taught myself how to play guitar. I was running 14 miles every three days. I also began to read the books that I have and bought more and I was having fun.

I felt so good that I got approval from my doctor and went back to work for the local government entity. I got a job with the Aviation department. I was the archivist for the history of the airport. It was an interesting job. I had to build a program. It was stressful, but rewarding.

This job however, began to take away my energy and depleted my efforts that were focused on accomplishing my goals. I became sick again. I went to different doctors and got even stronger medicine. I got so sick that I ended up in a wheelchair completely unable to walk for two years. I was a zombie. By this point, I was no longer working on my goals and I had thoughts of committing suicide once again. I spent another week in the hospital.

This behavior continued for a while. Until, one day, I decided that this was enough. I no longer had a purpose. I was just existing and I knew that wasn't right. I did have a purpose and had to get back on track.

While I was in the chair I gained 70 pounds from lack of movement and the medication. I decided that I needed to lose the weight, get out of the chair and off of the medication. Once I did that, I would write another plan and get back on track.

I began by forcing myself out of the wheel chair. After several months, I lost over 60 pounds. After working on those things for six months, I decided it was time to get off of all of my medication completely and for good.

So, one day I quit taking all of it, cold turkey. The next seven days were pure hell. I had hallucinations, vomiting, chills, fever and I couldn't sleep. An hour seemed like a day and a few days seemed like months. But, I was driven. I would get through this and serve my purpose.

After that week, things started to improve for me. After two months of being completely off of my medicine, I went to the doctor. I brought all of my unfinished medicine with me and dropped it all on her desk and said, "That is it. I am done!" You can imagine her reaction. She was happy for me and very supportive.

After that, I started focusing on what I want to really do in life and what my purpose is. I got up one morning and packed some things after Frida went to work. I then left the house and went to a hotel. I could not live there anymore. It was a bad place for me. I figured she would either eventually join me where ever I was or that would be the end of things for us. But, I had to move forward.

Eventually, she agreed and we found a new place to live. I moved in immediately and she moved in a couple of months later. While I was there, I began to make my plan and enact it. After a few months, I came up with a new plan and enacted it. I am now producing and writing my books and setting up a program to help other veterans and people in general to heal from their past and move forward with their lives. Thus, helping them to also fulfill their purpose.

I also made some investments in the stock market. I made plans for, and began working towards, having my own restaurant and vineyard and acquiring some real estate and rental properties. I contacted all of my old friends from my child hood and got back in touch with them as well as with my father.

My new plan now looks like this:

1. I will write and publish four books
2. I will invest $100,000.00 in the stock market
3. I will acquire three rental properties
4. I will open my own restaurant
5. I will earn $89,000.00 a month this upcoming year

6. I will lose 15 more pounds and I will be healthy
7. I will have a new vehicle to my liking
8. I will have a high rise home in downtown San Diego, a log cabin home up north in the woods with a lot of trees and a stream, and I will have a home in the desert with stunning views
9. I will have built a stellar wine collection
10. I will have started my own vineyard

I work on all of these goals each and every day. I am on fire! I can and will do this and not only enhance my life, but enhance other people's lives through the accomplishment of my goals. I know that there are no limitations. I can do whatever I wish to do. My mind is my only limitation. So, I will change the way I think and create what I want internally in my mind so that it will manifest itself physically in my life. I also study every day. Knowledge is the best way to limit risk and loss. There is no excuse now a days for not being informed. Knowledge is everywhere and at your fingertips. I do things everyday towards accomplishing my goals and I don't waste time on anything else that has nothing to do with their attainment.

I have arrived at this point in January of 2014. I started this journey in 2008. What a ride! If I can do this after going through everything I have gone through and fought through, so can you! There are no excuses. Remember, that no matter what, "Always, always, always move forward!" "Learn to heal from your past, become inspired, move forward and BE successful with your lives!" Amen!

The end.

Copyright 2014 Robert A. Serocki, Jr.

Robert Serocki, Jr. has a bachelor's degree in Anthropology, with an Emphasis on Archaeology, from Arizona State University. He was a professional archaeologist for nearly 20 years. He now is a full time author (www.robertserocki.com) and stock market investor. This is his second publication and he is now writing his third book. He also currently participates in a creative writing group at his local Veterans Administration Hospital helping veterans to heal from their grief and has plans to develop his own program to help others heal and become successful with their lives.

www.ingramcontent.com/pod-product-compliance
Lightning Source LLC
Chambersburg PA
CBHW052052070526
44584CB00017B/2150